THE ESSENTIAL LITTLE
CRUISE BOOK

"Cruisers will find noteworthy nuggets in
The Essential Little Cruise Book by
veteran cruise director Jim West."

—*New York Post*

"Nuggets of wisdom from a veteran cruise
director . . . a real charmer."

—*Chicago Tribune*

"A pocket-sized treasure-trove of tips for both
first-time cruisers and old salts."

—Charles Doherty, managing editor,
Cruise Travel Magazine

"A store of helpful hints to make your journey
aboard a cruise ship smooth sailing all the way."

—*Navy Times*

THE ESSENTIAL LITTLE
CRUISE BOOK

Secrets from a
Cruise Director for a Perfect
Cruise Vacation

THIRD EDITION

Jim West

The
Globe
Pequot
Press

GUILFORD, CONNECTICUT

Text design by Joanna Beyer

ISBN 0-7627-2828-0

Manufactured in the United States of America
Third Edition/First Printing

*This book is dedicated to
Lucille (Grandma) West, who bought me a sailor suit
when I was two years old. Who would have thought?!*

Contents

Acknowledgments

I wish first to thank God for giving me so many wonderful opportunities: to explore the planet, to meet fascinating people, and to discover more about myself. My cruise adventures and life adventure have been absolutely brilliant thus far.

I thank my family: My mother and father, who taught me the value of being a good, honest, and decent person. My brothers, Michael and Ricky, and my sisters, Laurie and Marysue, who listened to my countless cruise stories with genuine interest.

I also would like to thank my staff for their hard work and dedication to my goals. Many thanks to my colleagues at Princess Cruises, Celebrity Cruises, and Orient Lines, who gave me the opportunity to work with their companies.

I am also grateful to Sir Edmund and Lady June Hillary, to my friends at many of the other cruise lines, and especially to Bret Bullock and to Ditmar Wertanzl (Crystal Cruises), who believed I could be a cruise director and then opened the door.

And finally, it is with great appreciation and fondness that I thank the one million cruise passengers I have sailed with over the years. God bless.

Introduction

I first began working on cruise ships (the *original* Dawn Princess) fifteen years ago. Since then I have sailed on more than eight hundred cruises and have had the unique opportunity to talk with over one million cruise passengers, from families and seniors to singles and corporate travelers. Early in my career as a cruise director, I noticed that many passengers were desperate for information that would make their cruise a success. Many of them made comments like, "If only we had known this before we left home!" or "Why didn't my cruise agent prepare me for this?" The same questions and concerns arose time and again. I began to keep a journal, noting the issues and concerns that were especially important to passengers. This book evolved as a result.

Of course, no matter how good the cruise line, no one can take you by the hand and explain every last detail about a cruise. Each and every voyage is different—the officers, staff, and crew onboard the ship; the passengers sailing on that particular voyage; weather conditions; the ship itself; and how much information your cruise agent has given you are all important factors in determining the success of a cruise. But, that said, it is also true that a few tips can help to smooth the cruising waters. Whether you are planning your first voyage or your tenth, the tips and suggestions provided here can make the difference between having a good cruise and having an excellent cruise.

Since writing the second edition of this book, many changes have occurred in the cruise industry. Large cruise lines have merged, have been purchased, or are no longer in business. The threat of terrorist attacks on cruise ships has put safety and security measures at an all-time high. The Norwalk virus and other illnesses that have occurred onboard some ships have caused concern to some cruisers. With all this said, a cruise still remains the best vacation and best value for your vacation dollar, as the number of cruisers in North America reaches over ten million.

Cruise lines have learned it is more important to offer a low cruise rate to fill their ships than to have their ships sail half empty, with the idea that once you're onboard you'll spend money. And so, the cost of a cruise vacation is lower than it's ever been.

In this new edition of my book, I've included some terrific Web sites that I hope will provide you with ways to save money and enhance your cruise experience. One of the best resources I've found is the Cruise Yellow Pages. It lists every possible company that has anything to do with cruising. The Web site is www.cruiseyellowpages.com. Also, I've added a new section that will specifically assist Alaska cruisers and Caribbean cruisers on their voyages.

It's been said that a cruise is what *you* make it. You'll be presented with an opportunity to let your senses run wild. Enjoy the ride.

FIRST THINGS FIRST: CHOOSING A CRUISE

MILLIONS OF PEOPLE HAVE ALREADY experienced the joy in going on a cruise. Cruise lines offer an exciting array of cruise "products" today, and it takes only the skilled juggling of a travel planner to match your personality and budget with the cruise line, cruise ship, and itinerary that suit your needs. One of the most important things to remember when planning your cruise is to gather as much information as you can *before* you reach into your wallet and dish out money. Having the right information beforehand will prevent problems from occurring and eliminate unpleasant surprises once you arrive onboard the ship.

Cruise ships are often referred to as "floating resorts" or "floating hotels," since your life is centered on the vessel for the duration of the cruise. Thus, it's essential that you become familiar with the amenities that a particular ship and cruise line have to offer. You won't want to be booked on a cruise with a family-oriented theme if you are single

2 and looking to party hearty. If you hate sunny, hot weather, you'll be happier cruising in Alaska or Canada than to the Caribbean. And if you don't like crowds or glitz, a freighter that accommodates only twelve passengers may please you more than a huge, modern cruise ship that draws a couple of thousand.

DOING YOUR HOMEWORK

Think of preparing for your cruise as if you were preparing for a test at school. You can do just enough work to make a passing grade, or you can do a more thorough research job and score an A+—which translates into an excellent vacation! Even if you're a frequent cruiser, there are always new things to learn.

The best sources of information about cruising are cruise agents, friends and family who have gone on cruises, travel books and magazines, and the Internet. Ask questions and keep notes about what you learn. First-time cruisers have hundreds of questions pertaining to their cruise. If you're looking for personal service and information on ways to get

the most out of your first cruise, contact the people   3
at www.cruisestaff.com and let them help you plan
each step of your cruise with the utmost care. It's
often better service than your local cruise agent
could ever possibly give you.

There are many cruise Web sites that offer cruise
pricing. To avoid becoming overwhelmed with all
that's out there in Cyberland, start with www.cruise
group.com. Ten of the top cruise Web sites are
located under one domain name. Each Web site
offers different services to people from all walks of
life.

Many of the large Internet travel companies are
eager to provide cruise prices and make your
reservation, but they are not always available to
assist if you encounter a problem. It's always good
to compare prices, but I would make cruise reservations with a Web site recommended in this book.

They advertise themselves as being the *"Internet
Web site that cruise lines and travel agents hope
you never find."* You can obtain a cruise refund,

4 perhaps hundreds of dollars, simply by granting www.cruiserebate.com permission to take over your booking. For anyone who has made cruise reservations directly with the cruise line or onboard a cruise ship, this Web site is highly recommended as a great way to save even more money.

Be aware that not all Internet Web sites are secure. Before you pay for your cruise using your credit card, make sure the company confirms that its Web site is secure and no hackers are able to retrieve your credit card number.

Cruise prices that appear in the travel section of a Sunday newspaper are usually not the actual price you'll finally pay for your cruise. Read the small print at the bottom of the page and be sure the price includes port charges, accommodations, and all taxes.

If you have made your air arrangements to and from the ship through the cruise line, ask your cruise agent to contact the line about a schedule that suits your needs. This usually costs $50 per person and there may be some additional costs from the airline.

Most shore excursions can be booked in advance through the cruise line's Web site. Obtain your reservation or booking number from your cruise agent to use when you confirm your tours.

To purchase a videotape of the cruise you are planning, contact Video Cruises, Inc. at (815) 878–3600 or log onto the Web site at www.video cruises.com. The cost for each video is approximately $15.

WHERE TO GO?

One of the questions that I am asked most often is, "Where is the best place to cruise?" My standard answer? "Cruise anywhere, anytime, anyplace! Your worst day on a cruise ship is better than your best day at work!"

Cruise passengers are becoming more adventurous about exploring Planet Earth. Now that more and more people are testing the cruising

6

waters, cruise lines have become enthusiastic about sailing to new and exciting ports of call. The Mediterranean Sea, Baltic Sea, Canary Islands, Red Sea, Indian Ocean, Southeast Asia, Amazon River, the South Seas, and even Antarctica are quickly becoming popular cruise areas. Who would have thought even twenty years ago that you could explore so many remote areas of the world in comfort and luxury, and at such affordable prices?

There are a number of cruise lines operating in all different parts of the world. For space reasons, however, I cannot list them here. Your travel agent (especially an agent that specializes in cruise travel) is the best source of information on which lines sail to which regions.

Check with your local library or bookstore for general information and the history of the ports of call your ship will be visiting. You will have a better understanding and appreciation of each locale when the ship docks and you begin exploring.

The people you meet in the different ports of call   7
are one of the things that you will remember most
about your vacation. Cruise in an area where the
people have a reputation for being friendly and
polite to tourists.

A cruise that stops at more ports of call does not
necessarily mean a better cruise. Keep in mind that
an endless round of ports can become tedious.
And many passengers enjoy being at sea as much
as, if not more than, being on land.

Unless you have been on a number of cruises and
proved to have exceptional stamina, look for a
cruise itinerary that is not too demanding, especially if you are not able to walk around easily.

CARIBBEAN CRUISE TIPS

*The Caribbean is to North Americans as the
Mediterranean is to Europeans. It's an exciting
cruise vacation destination that's close and fun
and offers many things to many passengers. Who
can resist sailing onboard a cruise ship in eighty-*

8   *five-degree weather in the middle of winter, while enjoying an array of sightseeing and historic attractions? Whether you're snorkeling with the stingrays in the Grand Cayman, looking at the stalagmites inside a cave in Barbados, or simply basking nude in the sun on a beach in St. Martin, your Caribbean cruise will offer all kinds of exciting things to do and see.*

Cruise ships in the Caribbean are designed to provide a variety of options to singles, families, gays and lesbians, seniors, honeymooners, and anyone else looking for an exciting vacation that's relaxing and fun. From rock-climbing walls and topless sundecks to state-of-the-art health clubs and private dining rooms, cruise ships in the Caribbean offer it all. Here are just a few tips for getting the most out of your Caribbean cruise.

The Caribbean islands consist of a full range of sizes and exotic backgrounds. Your Caribbean cruise will offer a diverse cross section of cultures in a short amount of time. Sample and taste it all!

Caribbean cruises come in all shapes and sizes and can last two, three, four, five, seven, eight, ten, twelve, and fourteen days on all kinds of vessels, large and small. Sometimes a cruise line offers a better cruise value on a seven-day itinerary than on a four-day. Have your cruise agent find you the best value before you make your deposit.

Cruise ships that sail to the Caribbean can originate from many U.S. cities: Fort Lauderdale, Miami, Tampa, New Orleans, Galveston, Baltimore, Philadelphia, and New York City, to name a few. Have your cruise agent price the different locations in the event the cruise line offers a "resident" or "senior" rate.

Tourist season in the Caribbean for "land" vacationers is from mid-December to mid-April. If you want to cruise when it's less crowded in the ports, opt to cruise from mid-April to mid-December.

The newest and largest cruise ships in the world sail in the Caribbean, primarily because of their size and also because the Caribbean is such a popular destination. The larger the ship, the more options there are for groups traveling together.

10   A back-to-back cruise, alternating the eastern and western Caribbean itineraries, is a wonderful way to relax and enjoy a longer cruise. Have your cruise agent negotiate a good cruise fare. Be sure your cabin location is confirmed in writing and that you are allowed to stay in the same stateroom for both cruises.

You can save money on airfare if your cruise begins in either the *eastern* Caribbean (Bahamas) or *western* Caribbean (Mexico), as opposed to the southern Caribbean, in San Juan, Puerto Rico.

No vaccinations are required to sail on a Caribbean cruise.

Disney Cruise Lines offers some wonderful family cruise and land packages to the Caribbean. If you are interested, have your cruise agent price Disney's land and sea package and then select another cruise line with your Disney land package to see where the best value lies. You may not have to keep the entire vacation with Disney because other cruise lines might offer a better price for the cruise portion of your vacation.

Because cruise ships stop in many remote ports in the Caribbean, federal authorities are always looking for drug trafficking. Guard dogs are usually on the gangway when the ship returns to sniff out the drug dealers.

Hurricane season in the Caribbean is September through November, but don't let that scare you from booking a cruise during this time of year. Cruise lines offer incredible rates on these cruises and the captains of the ships have advance notice to avoid any problems with the weather.

The Caribbean is the number one cruise destination for families during the summer months and holidays. If you don't want to sail on a cruise ship buzzing with children, opt for an alternative date to cruise.

12 There is a tendency to overpack for most cruises, especially a Caribbean cruise. Realistically, you'll be in shorts, swimsuit, T-shirt, tennis shoes, sandals, or your bare feet most of the time. It's very casual during the daytime. For evening attire, have your cruise agent suggest some options so you don't get too carried away with your packing.

Even though a Caribbean cruise provides an opportunity to enjoy warm weather, pack a sweater. Sometimes the lounges and public rooms on the ship have the air-conditioning set too cold, and you'll need some sort of cover-up.

When you are shopping in the Caribbean and you hear that the port is "duty-free," this means no taxes are added to any of your purchases.

United States Customs allows up to $400 worth of goods per person to be brought back into the country duty-free. Anything over that allotment will be assessed a charge. If you make a large purchase in the Caribbean, use your credit card and be sure to ask the store clerk to ship your merchan-

dise home. This is the best way to avoid a customs   13
penalty.

Call your credit card company *before* you leave home and let them know you'll be cruising in the Caribbean. Sometimes credit card companies put a stop on purchases if there is a sudden burst of charges from a location other than your normal shopping places at home.

The U.S. dollar is widely accepted throughout the entire Caribbean. It is always a good idea to have at least $20 in single dollar bills each time you visit a new port in the event the people you are dealing with cannot make change.

Traveler's checks are rarely used in the Caribbean. In fact, they've become more of a burden than a protection. ATM machines are located on nearly all ships and in the ports of call. You should consider using your credit card for nearly all your purchases.

Be out on the open decks as the ship pulls in and out of port. Quite often the cruise lines have hired

14 local dancers or calypso bands to play Caribbean music as part of their welcome and farewell.

Some Caribbean cruises include the Panama Canal in their itinerary. The morning the ship goes through the canal be sure you are on the top deck toward the front. You'll have the best view of how the canal operates.

Find out ahead of time if your cruise ship stops in port on a Sunday or local holiday. In some cases, the shops and attractions will be closed and there will be nothing to do in the town, so you might want to book a shore excursion on that day.

To enhance your time in each port of call, contact the tourist board in each place your ship will be docking or look on the Internet. You'll find things the cruise line's shore excursion department will not be promoting or mentioning.

Taxi drivers on many Caribbean islands negotiate prices. Be sure both you *and* the taxi driver are clear on the rate before you start. If you are taking a taxi to a particular beach, negotiate the price and the time the taxi driver will return and bring you back to the ship. *Pay the taxi driver only upon returning to the ship.* This ensures that the taxi driver will come back to pick you up. Otherwise, you may be stranded on a beach with no transportation.

If you are planning to take an interisland ferry to visit a neighboring island, allow plenty of time to return to the ship. If the ferry is delayed or has mechanical problems, have a backup plan to get you to the ship before it sails.

If you miss the ship and it sails to the next island without you, contact the cruise line's port agent for assistance. They can help you with transportation to your next port of call. And, this is all at *your* expense.

The island of St. Maarten/St. Martin offers a Dutch side and a French side. If you decide to visit Orient Beach, the nude beach, plan on taking your clothes off. The locals will ask you to leave if you're there to just gawk or take photographs.

16 If your cruise visits Barbados, be sure to sample the flying fish sandwich. It's excellent and it's an island specialty.

Some ports in the Caribbean offer casinos. It's unlikely the slot machines are set to pay much money, since most of the people who go into them are cruise passengers and not locals. If you want to gamble, wait until you get back onboard the ship.

If your cruise originates in San Juan, Puerto Rico, fly out a day or so before your cruise begins. You'll have some time to enjoy Old San Juan or the rain forest or maybe even recapture any luggage the airline might have misplaced.

Without doubt, St. Thomas is the shopping capital of the entire Caribbean. If you are traveling with family members, purchase a set of walkie-talkies so you can communicate with each other in the midst of the 600 shops and restaurants. You might even purchase them there, since everything is duty free.

St. Thomas offers all kinds of jewelry shops. You 17 can negotiate the best deal if you play one against the other. Suddenly that 5 percent discount they first offered you turns into a 25 percent discount just because you mentioned you were interested in their competitor's jewelry. This basically applies to all purchases.

One of the best souvenirs you can bring back from a cruise in the Caribbean is rum cake from the Cayman Islands. These cakes come in all sizes and prices and are vacuum-sealed so they will pass through U.S. Customs. You'll find them in many ports of call.

Certain animal items such as tortoise shells are not allowed into the United States. Avoid purchasing any of these items, as they will be confiscated by Customs authorities and you'll receive a hefty fine.

Scuba divers will have a great experience in many Caribbean ports. If you're planning to dive, be sure to bring your scuba certification and dive log. You

18   will not be allowed to rent dive equipment if you forget your documents.

If you have never snorkeled, or even if you have, don't pass up this opportunity. It will be one of the most memorable experiences of your cruise. Be sure to buy an underwater camera for some exciting photographs.

The Caribbean sun and clouds can be deceiving. Always wear some kind of sunblock, even if you don't think you'll get burned. Believe me, it's when you don't think you'll get zapped that you really do.

The Caribbean sun and clouds can be deceiving. Always wear some kind of sunblock, even if you don't think you'll get burned. Believe me, it's when you don't think you'll get zapped that you really do.

Humidity is high in the Caribbean during the summer months. If the lens of your video camera begins to fog when you walk outside from an air-conditioned room on the ship, wait fifteen minutes or so and allow the camera time to defog.

The food is exotic and savory in many of the local restaurants in port. Be sure you've packed something to take should any irregularities occur an hour or so after you eat.

Drink bottled water on the ship and in all the ports of call, no matter what you've heard about it being fine to drink.

Late-seating dining is usually the first to be wait-listed when cruising in the Caribbean. If this is important to you, have your cruise agent confirm your dinner reservations as soon as possible.

Sec

If you need to call home, wait until the ship arrives in one of the U.S. Virgin Islands. The telephones are just like those at home, and it will be much easier and less expensive to call from there.

ALASKA CRUISE TIPS

When my publisher asked me to add a section of Alaska cruise tips to this new edition of my book, I was thrilled. Having sailed on over one hundred Alaska cruises, I can honestly say this is one area

20 *of the world I know better than any other cruise destination. The only problem I had was deciding which tips to include and which to leave out. The following are what I feel are the most important for you to know before you go.*

The options available for cruising in Alaska range from small expedition ships to large ocean liners. It might be wise to look into all the options before you make a final decision. Normally, the smaller the ship, the more expensive the Alaska cruise.

When you are selecting an outside cabin for your Alaska cruise and your ship is sailing northbound, have your cruise agent choose a cabin on the starboard (right) side of the ship and vice versa for southbound cruises. This will provide better scenery for the entire cruise.

The type of ship you choose is important to the success of your Alaska cruise. Unless your cruise agent is experienced with Alaska cruising, you may end up with a ship and cruise line that are not providing the type of cruise that best suits your needs. Do your homework and don't settle for just a regular travel agent's advice.

The smaller cruise ships in Alaska do not provide the medical assistance that the larger ocean liners provide. If you require special medical assistance or if you like the idea of a full hospital facility onboard your ship, opt for the larger, newer vessels instead of the smaller ships.

Because Alaska is so different from any other cruise destination and the scenery so spectacular, it's worth upgrading your cabin to a balcony or, at the very least, a window. You'll have no regrets paying the extra money.

If you are sailing either northbound or southbound and you need to transfer between Anchorage and Seward, ask your cruise agent to check the availability and pricing of a train ride as opposed to a motorcoach transfer. This will make the three-hour journey more exciting and fun.

22   If you are looking at an Alaska brochure from the cruise lines, don't let their prices scare. Cruise agents and Internet companies receive all kinds of great deals, so see what prices they can offer you. It's unlikely you'll ever pay the rates that are listed in their brochures.

Packing for your Alaska cruise is unlike packing for any other cruise. Because the weather is unpredictable, you have to pack for cold, warm, and rainy weather. Layering your clothing is the best way to avoid overpacking. Start with the heavier clothing and work your way to a lightweight waterproof jacket.

Essentials to pack for your Alaska cruise are lightweight raincoat, umbrella, binoculars, backpack, sweater, and comfortable shoes.

Pack a swimsuit even on an Alaska cruise. The temperature can sometimes reach eighty degrees during the summer months. You may even be tempted to swim in the swimming pool or relax in the Jacuzzi.

Whether you start your cruise in Anchorage, Vancouver, Fairbanks, or Seattle, and you need to fly to your port of embarkation, make arrangements to arrive a day prior to your cruise. This will give you an opportunity to see that city and retrieve any lost luggage in the event the airline loses a piece.

If you plan on staying a night in Vancouver *prior* to your Alaska cruise, a good place to stay is the Pan Pacific Hotel, located at Canada Place. It's a 5-star property, in an excellent location. One of the services they offer is transferring your luggage directly to your cruise ship the morning of embarkation. For more information contact Cruise Hotels, toll-free at (888) 867–8600.

Vancouver is one of the best cities in the world, offering an assortment of things to do. Visit Gastown, Stanley Park, Granville Island, Queen Elizabeth Gardens, and Chinatown. You'll find exquisite shopping on Robson Street and a wide variety of restaurants to choose from.

Seattle is not only a contemporary city, but there

24 are some terrific tours to participate in as well. I recommend a day trip to Mt. Rainier, a boat ride through the Hiram Chittenden Locks, the Space Needle, and a city tour with Gray Line Tours.

❂

Alaska is in the Pacific Northwest of the United States—be prepared for rain every day of your Alaska cruise, no matter what month you go. If there is a day it doesn't rain, consider it a gift from God.

❂

It's been said that the summer months are the best time to see Alaska. There is no guarantee it won't rain during this time and, because it's peak season, you'll pay a higher price for your cruise. If you're flexible and can sail in mid-May or mid-September, you'll find a much better deal for your cruise.

❂

The difference between an Alaska cruise and an Alaska cruise tour is that a cruise tour includes a land package in Denali Park. If you opt for the tour, plan on spending at least $1,000 more per person for your package.

If you are interested only in a seven-day cruise and not the Denali land tour and you want to save money on airfare, book an Alaska cruise that originates and ends in the same port of call.

If you are interested in adding a Denali Park land package onto your cruise and you don't want to pay the high prices the cruise lines charge, contact www.denalicruisetours.com for more information.

Another option for your Alaska cruise is to include the Canadian Rockies before or after your cruise. This includes traveling into the Canadian Rocky Mountains to Calgary, Banff, and Jasper. It's spectacular scenery and different from Alaska.

Wildlife will be abundant on your Alaska cruise. Early morning and early evening are when birds and animals are most active, so be out on the top deck of the ship so you look on both sides.

When the ship sails into Glacier Bay, be outside toward the front of the ship. Quite often you'll see

26   harbor seals relaxing on icebergs that have calved off the glacier ahead.

It's easy to spot bald eagles on your Alaska cruise. Look for something resembling a white golf ball in the trees—this will be the crown of the bald eagle— then get a closer look with your binoculars.

It's easy to spot bald eagles on your Alaska cruise.

Humpback, orca, and beluga whales can be found in the Inside Passage. They are usually in calm waters, so it should be easy to see them spouting and breaching out of the water.

When cruising through the Inside Passage, cruise lines hire park rangers who narrate the sights over the PA system out on the open decks. Be sure you are outside and available to walk to either side of the ship when they spot some wildlife.

When you see the glaciers for the first time, it's likely your breath will be taken away. It's a sight you'll never forget. Don't get too involved in video-taping it; you'll miss everything else around you if

you do. The ship will sell videos of the glaciers, so 27
you can still take home a good souvenir.

One of the best occasions for a photograph is the day the ship sails into Glacier Bay. If you are cruising with a group, arrange a meeting with the ship's photographer outside on the deck for that magic Kodak moment.

If it's raining on the day your ship sails into Glacier Bay and you don't want to stand outside with your umbrella, the next best place to be is toward the front of the ship in a lounge that has a lot of windows. Otherwise, a comfortable seat next to the window in the upstairs buffet restaurant will do just fine.

Many Alaska shore excursions sell out before the ship even sails because passengers have booked them ahead of time on the Internet. If there are some shore excursions you don't want to miss, make your reservations in advance. Your cruise agent can assist you with this.

28 Juneau is the capital of Alaska and provides all kinds of shore excursions and tours. I recommend a visit to the Mendenhal Glacier by helicopter, a stop at the Red Dog Saloon, or a ride on the Mount Roberts Tramway to see breathtaking views 1,700 feet above sea level.

One of my favorite tours in Juneau is to the Taku Glacier Lodge. You'll enjoy a flight over snow-capped mountains, the picturesque setting near Taku Glacier, and a terrific salmon lunch, and you may even have the opportunity to see some of the local bears. This tour sells out, so make your reservations well in advance.

Don't miss the bronze statue in Juneau dedicated to Patsy Ann, the dog that greeted fortune seekers back in the gold rush days.

In Ketchikan, a visit to Creek Street will provide some interesting shopping in the small boutique shops built on pilings. The main attraction is the famous Dolly's House Museum. You'll understand

why Creek Street was the place fish and fishermen
went to spawn.

At certain times of the year, the creek at Creek Street is filled with salmon swimming upstream to lay their eggs. Be sure to bring your camera—it's an amazing sight.

One of the more popular things to do in Ketchikan is see the Great Alaska Lumberjack Show. You can purchase your tickets onboard the ship or at the location itself, which is just walking distance from most ships. It's a fun family show and great entertainment for all ages.

If you plan on buying smoked salmon in Ketchikan, be sure you've shopped around at different stores in town before you make your purchase. The prices can vary by $10 for different brands and salmon type.

At the Deer Creek Hatchery in Ketchikan you'll see up close the fascinating behavior of salmon.

30   Ketchikan receives over 162 inches of rain a year, so be prepared for liquid sunshine.

Sportfishing is available in Juneau and Ketchikan and is usually a five-hour tour. This excursion can be booked through the cruise line or directly with some of the fishermen in port. The price includes poles, bait, boat, guide, and fishing license.

When exploring Anchorage, the place to begin is the Log Cabin Visitor Information Center. You'll receive information about restaurants, art galleries, museums, and events happening around the city.

If you participate in any of the Salmon Bake Tours, be sure to ask if you'll be eating indoors or outdoors. If you eat outdoors, Alaska's unofficial state "bird," the mosquito, might be a problem unless you're wearing some kind of repellent. Don't forget to pack some.

When cruising in and out of Sitka, it's possible the ship might experience rough weather, being farther from the coast. If you are prone to motion sickness, be sure you've taken some medication an hour or so before the ship sails in or out of that port.

Skagway is the gateway to the Klondike goldfield. Before you begin walking around town, make a stop in the visitor center and watch a short film about its history. It will give you a better appreciation of the town.

Just outside the city limits of Skagway lies the Gold Rush Cemetery with all its famous characters from the days of '98 laid to rest. It's fun to read the headstones and recall the excitement and thrill of what once was.

One of the most exciting and certainly one of the most expensive shore excursions in Skagway is the Pilots Choice helicopter ride, where you actually land on a glacier and walk around. If your budget can handle the cost and you're not afraid to ride in a helicopter, it will be an unforgettable experience.

32 Haines is a small town near Skagway that has a large concentration of bald eagles. If your cruise ship is stopping there, be ready with your binoculars. This is also a great spot to take photographs of snowcapped mountains.

The White Pass Railway in Skagway is a must, especially if you are not going to Denali Park on the train. It follows the original trail the gold miners used and the scenery is extraordinary. Be sure you sit facing forward on the left side of the train. You'll capture more scenery.

If you are interested in seeing the world's largest collection of totem poles and learning about the Tlingit Indians, the Saxman Village or the Totem Heritage Center tours are not to be missed. These shore excursions are offered by nearly all the cruise lines.

You can get great shopping bargains toward the end of the tourist or cruising season. By mid-September in Alaska you might get 50 to 75 percent off.

The United States Customs authorities and Canadian authorities have strict regulations that state no arts and crafts objects made from body parts of animals are allowed to enter the country. If you plan on purchasing any items made of walrus tusks, scrimshaw, or whale bones, have the shop mail these items directly to your home.

Whenever you are hiking through the woods on your own, be sure to carry a bell or sing loudly as you walk. It might seem a little odd, but bears will run away if they hear you approaching. Bears will attack when they feel threatened or are taken by surprise.

You might consider reading a few books or watching a few movies about Alaska before you sail. It makes the experience more fulfilling.

SIZE MATTERS!

Like people, cruise ships come in all sorts of shapes and sizes. Some are classy, with sleek lines, while others are somewhat brassy. Some

34 *are huge and a bit show-offish, some very romantic and intimate, and others just efficient and functional. A larger ship is not necessarily a better ship—and vice versa. Your personal preferences as to size and other defining characteristics of a ship, such as age, should dictate your choice.*

Think of a large ship as a floating resort and a small ship as a floating inn or hotel.

The smaller the ship, the more intimate the surroundings and personalized the service on the cruise. It is also likely to be more expensive. These types of cruises tend to attract older and more sophisticated travelers.

Smaller ships provide quick and easy disembarkation when the ship is docked in port, not to mention on the final day of the cruise.

Generally speaking, the smaller the ship, the more the cruise line has focused on the ports of call and shore excursion program.

The promenade deck on a larger cruise ship completely wraps around the ship, whereas the promenade deck on a smaller vessel may wrap around only three sides.

Larger vessels, for the most part, have more people, more noise, and more activities.

The larger cruise ships provide a greater assortment of activities and entertainment for passengers of all ages.

Generally speaking, the larger the ship, the more lavish the production shows, casino, swimming pools, health club and spa, and sunbathing areas.

The larger the ship, the greater the chance that you will be tendered ashore in smaller boats.

Sometimes the size of the ship is less important than the age of the ship. New ships offer the latest technology, with conference rooms and computers that are connected to the Internet, interactive

36 television, enormous playrooms for children, and state-of-the-art health and beauty facilities. The cabins are fresh and more attractive, and the shower stalls are comfortably sized. The public rooms provide more space, and the entire ship is made to accommodate large groups of people. Nearly all the major lounges are wheelchair accessible, and the ships boast more sophisticated safety systems.

Many older ships have larger cabins with more closet and drawer space. These ships can withstand a storm better than some newer ships because they were constructed with deeper drafts. There are usually more intimate spaces available in the public areas, and there are more classic nautical lines and wood inlays, as opposed to neon lights and water slides.

The maiden voyage of a cruise ship is exciting, but problems are inevitable. Don't expect everything to be perfect. As with all things that are brand new, it takes some time before the kinks are worked out. Wait a couple of months, then sail.

TYPES OF CRUISES

The cruise industry, more than any other segment of the travel industry, boasts a nearly endless variety of options for travelers. When they hear the word cruise, *most people immediately think of coastal voyages. But there are also riverboat and river barge trips, round-the-world cruises, tall sailing-ship cruises, freighter and cargo-ship cruises crossing from one continent to another, and special expedition cruises. While they are all different, each of these specialty cruises offers a great opportunity for vacationing on a ship.*

Cruise passengers come in all shapes, sizes, and appearances. Cruise Concepts, Inc. is a company specializing in nude cruises. For more information call (815) 878–3600.

Special educational cruises are available through some cruise lines. How about traveling to the Galapagos with a team of biologists and oceanographers? Or cruising to ports in Greece and Turkey with a group of archaeologists? Not only will you

38 get to visit exotic places, but you will learn a great
deal as well.

A cruise through the Panama Canal is not only
educational but will also give you the opportunity to
cruise in both the Caribbean and Pacific on the
same voyage. And you can get a great price if it's
a repositioning cruise from the Caribbean and
Alaska.

Many cruise ships sail to their own private islands.
These are wonderful places to just lie on the beach
and relax. Look for this special option in cruise itineraries.

A trans-Atlantic cruise is a seafaring adventure,
and one that is quite reasonable in price. (Before
undertaking this particular kind of cruise, however,
make sure you have your sea legs.) Trans-Atlantic
voyages involve five to eight days at sea with no
ports of call.

River barge cruises are ideal for people who are

afraid of the ocean, are afraid of getting seasick, or prefer a less hurried vacation.

Don't think of a barge cruise as sailing on a tug- boat. Many river barges are luxurious floating hotels, complete with elegant china, rich wood pan- eling, hot tubs, saunas, goose-down beds, and even fireplaces.

The obvious difference between cruising on a cruise ship and cruising on a river barge is the body of water on which you travel. A barge will cruise down charming narrow waterways and through can- als and enter areas of the world that cruise ships could never reach.

Cargo ships are very informal, so you do not need to pack any formal wear. One of the nice parts of cruising on a cargo ship is the constant interaction between the passengers and the officers onboard.

You will not find many organized activities on a cargo ship or freighter. It is a great place to write a

40   book, meditate, or just sit back and soak up the sun.

Passengers on a cargo ship are more relaxed, more flexible, and usually have more time to cruise.

A world cruise is one of the most prestigious adventures of all. These cruises often last for months, and the cost can easily reach $100,000 per person. The lines that offer world cruises also allow passengers to book just one portion or section of the cruise—a good way to meet fascinating seasoned travelers at a fraction of the time and cost of a true world cruise.

You may enjoy taking a theme cruise—perhaps one with sports celebrities, country western stars, jazz musicians, or even one that features rock oldies. Contact your cruise agent for a list and the dates of these cruises.

If you are an active person, a cruise onboard a sailing cruise ship may be just the ticket. Even though these ships are engine-powered for the most part,

the computerized sails are used from time to time.
These ships typically travel to more remote places
and offer exceptional shore adventure programs.

✦

The most fascinating and educational trips are the
expedition and nature cruises. These provide a
hands-on experience with wildlife, the environment,
and the sea. The prices for these cruises are higher
than for most other types, but they are well worth
the investment for those with adventurous spirits.

DETAILS, DETAILS:
PLANNING YOUR CRUISE

OK. YOU HAVE THOUGHT ABOUT WHAT part of the world you want to cruise in, the size of ship that appeals to you, and what type of cruise suits your needs and interests. Now it's time to start putting together the details that will form the basis of your wonderful cruise vacation.

THE PERFECT CRUISE AGENT

The basic element in a good cruise experience is having a good cruise agent. In planning a cruise, the right agent can save you literally hundreds of dollars, if not thousands. Forget riffling through the Sunday travel section of the newspaper and signing up directly with a cruise line that advertises a tempting bottom line (there are usually many restrictions and hidden costs). You need a cruise expert to arrange the cruise that's right for you.

The perfect cruise agent is one who has been on more than a dozen cruises, one who will not accept the first price offered by a cruise line, one who has

44   sailed with more than one cruise line, and one who provides more information than you ever thought possible.

There are three basic ways to make your cruise reservations: directly with the cruise line, through a cruise agent, or on the Internet. All three are fine, if you have enough information before you leave on your cruise. A frequent cruiser needs only a good cruise price, because previous experience will provide all the answers needed. The cruise line might offer some specials that the Internet companies are not aware of. A cruise agent is available to answer all the questions you might have and take care of any special requests you will need. However you make your reservations, be sure to check out all your options.

To determine if an agent is qualified to plan your cruise, ask a few pivotal questions: How many cruises have you personally been on? What makes you special as a cruise agent? Why do you feel you can provide a better cruise package than the competition? What cruise lines do you work with on a regular basis, and why? How many years have you been involved in the cruise industry?

Word of mouth is a great way to find a good cruise agent. Ask your friends, family, even business associates if they have any recommendations.

When considering working with a cruise agent, ask her for the names of several cruise clients who have used her services in the past. If she is reluctant to give you this information or makes any excuses, look for another agent.

Your dealings with a cruise agent should be fun— your relationship sets the tone for your vacation. If your personalities don't click early on, it's best to find another agent.

If the cruise agent you have chosen is insistent on one particular cruise line and does not offer any other suggestions, it may be that he receives a higher commission from that cruise line. Ask the agent to give you information about two or three

46 other cruise lines offering the same kind of product and price. If he doesn't seem enthusiastic, consider moving on to another agent who is interested in *your* needs rather than the commission.

A good cruise agent wants to do everything possible to plan the best cruise vacation for you, so give as much information as you possibly can. Be specific about how much money you are willing to spend, where you want to go, how long you want to travel, whether you want a quiet, relaxing cruise or an active one, and so on. In other words, do your homework before you walk into the cruise agency.

Ask your cruise agent to arrange the details for a special-occasion cruise. I can't think of a better place to celebrate a birthday, anniversary, graduation, family reunion, or maybe just the fact that you have enough sense to celebrate life! Cruise lines are happy to accommodate any special requests, within reason.

Cruise lines are very accommodating, especially when it comes to specific dietary needs. No matter if it's a salt-free, low-fat, or vegetarian diet, you'll have no problem receiving the dinner you are looking for. Make these arrangements beforehand with your cruise agent.

✦

Good cruise agents are worth their weight in gold. Once you've found one, show your appreciation with compliments, thank-you notes, and referrals.

QUALIFICATIONS TO LOOK FOR IN AN AGENT AND AGENCY

The way an agent and agency present themselves is exactly the way they will handle your cruise requests. Does your agent look sloppy and lack energy and details, or is she sharp and tailored, full of energy and a sense of humor? Is the agency cluttered, disorganized, with tatty, sun-bleached cruise-ship displays in the window, or does it look tidy and busy, with happy employees and customers?

Look for the CLIA (Cruise Lines International Association), ASTA (American Society of Travel Agents), NACOA (National Association of Cruise Oriented Agencies), or ARTA (Association of Retail Travel

48   Agents) emblem on the front door or window of the travel agency. This means that it is a legitimate agency.

❄

If a cruise agency in your area is aggressive in its promotions and advertising, chances are it will be just as vigorous in finding you the best deals on your cruise.

❄

Some cruise agencies place advertisements in newspapers or magazines, claiming to be the exclusive representative for a particular cruise line. Don't be fooled by these ads. No cruise line is exclusive to one travel agency.

SELECTING YOUR CABIN

Even if you expect to use your cabin just as a waystation—breezing in and out to catch a few z's and to shower—choosing the right one for you is an important part of planning your cruise. Your selection will affect not only the price but also the general tone of your adventure.

Think small. In fact, think very small. Don't expect your cabin to be as spacious as those pictured in

cruise-line brochures. (When they shoot the cabins
for brochures, photographers often use wide-angle
lenses that make them look larger than they are.)

View your cabin as you would your bedroom. How
big and fancy does it need to be? If the bare essentials of space and amenities will do, ask your cruise
agent to look for lower-cost options. If you typically
enjoy time spent in your hotel room as much as any
other part of a vacation, allocate a larger portion of
your budget to a more luxurious cabin.

Ask your cruise agent to inquire about the drawer
space, wardrobe space, and bathroom facilities in
the cabin you are thinking of booking. If you know
the actual dimensions, you won't be unpleasantly
surprised when you get on the ship.

If you book an outside cabin with a window (typically more expensive than an inside cabin), have
your cruise agent check the ship layout to make
sure that a lifeboat does not block the view—
unless, of course, you willingly receive a discount
on the cabin.

50 On many of the newer ships, the cabin size is the same whether you are on the fifth deck or the ninth (excluding the suites, of course). Why pay more for a higher deck that will increase your chances of getting seasick?

Beds onboard a ship are called berths. Some berths are side by side, and some are upper and lower. Ask your cruise agent to find out exactly where these berths are located in the cabin. Honeymoon couples and those seeking a little romance will not be too happy if the twin beds are bolted to the floor!

Avoid booking your cabin above or below the disco or above the propellers. There is a considerable amount of noise and vibration in these cabins.

If you can afford it, book a suite with a private verandah. You'll have delicious privacy while lying in the sun, viewing the scenery, and enjoying a private dinner.

When booking a private balcony, make sure it is private. On many ships, the balcony cabins are just below some of the main decks and passengers can look down onto your balcony.

Be aware that if you have a balcony cabin located just below the pool deck or sports deck you may get substantial noise from all the action above, plus the ship's workers cleaning late at night moving deck chairs around. It's recommended to obtain a balcony cabin that has cabins above and below.

Most cruise ships provide a shower facility, not a bathtub, in a standard cabin.

When money is no object, you might consider booking the penthouse suite on an upscale cruise line rather than a regular suite on a luxury line. This will give you your own personal cabin steward, butler, maid service, and plenty of luxurious extras. Plus, it will also get you a seat at the captain's table.

52 DISCOUNTS AND UPGRADES

When you are planning your cruise, remember that there are always ways to get a better fare than the first one quoted. Ask your cruise agent to really dig to find the best possible price. More times than not, the agent can obtain a discount or cabin upgrade for you simply by asking the district sales manager of the cruise line for help.

If you're looking for nothing but the lowest cruise fares possible, and you don't need the assistance of a cruise agent, contact www.greatcruisediscounts.com. Provide them with the specifics of what you're looking for and they'll give you a quote, all within minutes. It's also a wonderful place to learn about last-minute cruise specials.

If you have cruised in the past with a particular cruise line and are planning to book another cruise with the same company, ask your cruise agent to inquire about a free category upgrade for your next cruise. Cruise lines may accommodate such requests, providing the ship has available cabin space.

Cruise lines frequently offer two-for-one deals. If you come across any bargain rates—written or oral— ask your cruise agent to investigate. These deals are restricted to certain dates and ships, and a two-for-one rate is quoted from the prices listed in the brochure. Quite often these rates are *more* than what a last-minute discount would be.

Many cruise lines offer a discount for a third or fourth person traveling in your party, provided you all stay in the same cabin.

Cruise for free! Organize a group of sixteen people or more, and you can cruise for free. Your cruise agent can give you more information.

If you've ever thought of working as a cruise agent from your home, but you don't have a travel education or background, don't worry—www.cruisereferral. com offers 50 percent commission to you if you refer cruise clients to their Web site for business. It's also a great Web site if you go on a cruise and want the discount for yourself.

54 Some cruise lines allow children to cruise for free as long as they are staying in the same cabin as two adults who are paying a full cruise fare.

Cruise lines offer substantial discounts on their repositioning cruises—when a cruise ship is being moved, or repositioned, from one area of the world to another. The most common months for this are April and October.

Some cruise lines now offer the opportunity to charge your entire cruise vacation to a credit card provided by the cruise line. You are then allowed two to three years to pay for the entire vacation. Be careful, however, as the interest rates for these cards can be sky-high and you may end up paying more for your cruise.

Sometimes cruise lines offer promotional rates to single cruisers if they book at the last minute. Your cruise agent can help you with this.

If you book your cruise a year in advance, you could

receive a substantial discount. You will also be one of the first passengers considered if and when the ship offers any free cabin upgrades.

Cruise lines will occasionally offer a very low discounted price on a cruise a week or so before the ship departs. (If you have already purchased your ticket and the price of the discount is considerably less, it is unlikely you will be eligible for a refund.)

A back-to-back cruise is two consecutive cruises combined into one long one. Some cruise lines offer a substantial discount if you book this kind of trip. Back-to-back cruises are fun and provide wonderful prices if you have the time; however, there is no guarantee you will remain in the same cabin for both cruises. Your cruise agent should confirm this in writing from the cruise line before you leave.

For individuals or groups who are Christians, www. onholywaters.com is the cruise Web site worth checking out. This entire company is staffed by Christians who all provide great customer service

56 in addition to offering back to your church a per-
centage of the commission from your cruise.

If the cruise line terminates your cruise midway
through the voyage due to mechanical problems,
health concerns, and so on, it may be responsible
for providing you with a full refund. In most cases,
the refund will be made through your cruise agent.

BOOKING YOUR CRUISE

*Booking the cruise is the first big step to your adven-
ture. Make sure you have all the information beforehand—in writing—so that you feel comfortable paying
your deposit.*

Give your cruise agent ample time to find the best
price and the best ship for you. It takes a little extra
effort to design a good cruise package.

If you are booking your cruise through an Internet
company, be sure you have the name of the agent
who will be handling your cruise and his telephone

number in the event you have to call him because
you're having problems with the Internet.

If possible, book a one- or two-day prepackage
before your cruise. That way you have a couple
days to enjoy your port of embarkation before
departure. It also allows time for any lost luggage to
catch up with you.

Read all of the fine print in the "terms" portion of
the cruise ticket before paying for your cruise. If
there is anything you do not understand, have your
cruise agent explain it to you until it all makes
sense.

When a family is traveling together and two or three
cabins are reserved, the name of at least one adult
family member must be on each cabin. Once you
arrive onboard the ship, little is said if you change
the configuration to suit your family's needs.

If possible, pay for your cruise with a credit card. If

58 any problems arise, the credit-card company can assist in sorting out the situation.

Even if you have already placed your cruise deposit with a cruise agent, if a better deal comes along with another company for the exact same cruise, you *can* cancel your reservation with the original agent. But first make sure you are not under any penalty restrictions and that you have investigated the situation thoroughly. Contact www.cruiserebate.com for more information.

Port charges are added to the cost of the cruise and will be reflected in your cruise ticket. These typically are about $50 to $200 per person, depending on the itinerary.

If a two-category cabin upgrade is offered when you are booking your cruise, it may not be a better location than the original category. A midship cabin in a lower cabin category is preferable to a higher category cabin toward the front of the ship or above a noisy lounge.

If you book your own air transportation to the ship, 59
be sure not to book a return flight before 12:30 P.M.
If the disembarkation process is slow or delayed,
you may miss your flight, and the cruise line will not
be responsible for helping you reschedule another.

✿

Air-sea packages (which means you've purchased
your air tickets through the cruise line) give passengers free transfers to and from the ship.

TO INSURE, OR NOT TO INSURE?

*I always advise people to pay the extra money for
cruise insurance, no matter what your age. Life is
full of surprises, and sometimes people simply
must postpone their vacation. It is well worth the
relatively small insurance fee to guarantee a
refund in such cases.*

Most cruise lines offer insurance at a high rate
and do not cover lost luggage, missed cruise connection, or travel delay. The most reputable insurance company for cruises is Bon Voyage
Insurance. They work in conjunction with Access

60 America in protecting your cruise investment at a fraction of what the cruise lines charge for their coverage. For more information log onto their Web site at www.bonvoyageinsurance.com or call (888) 867–8600.

Some cruise lines offer insurance and promise to give you a refund no matter what reason you use to cancel. Be aware that this refund could be a future cruise credit with their cruise line and not actual money.

If you decide to cancel your cruise, you will receive a full credit only if you submit your notice in writing no later than two months prior to the day the ship departs. During holidays, this notice must be received in writing by the cruise line three months in advance.

Some travel-insurance companies have an exclusive family plan in which children sixteen years and younger receive full coverage at no additional charge, when accompanied by adults who purchase the policy.

You never know what type of medical emergency could occur on your vacation. Buy insurance that covers a medical emergency evacuation from the ship.

ON THE
ROAD TO THE
HIGH SEAS

THERE'S SOMETHING ABOUT GOING TO sea that makes people feel like they have to be more prepared than when they travel on land (or, for that matter, in the air). In actuality, the steps toward embarking on your cruise are much the same as going on any vacation. That said, however, it is also true that knowing what to expect and being well prepared will make your cruise that much more pleasant.

WHAT TO BRING?

They say that half the fun of going on a vacation is anticipating and planning it. Preparing your wardrobe and packing for the cruise are part of that fun. The bottom line: Don't get carried away! (Typically, first-time cruisers pack at least twice as many clothes as they need.) One or two bathing suits, a couple of shorts and shirts, a few sets of nice casual wear, and a couple of more dressy outfits should work out just fine. If you feel that you've underpacked (a rare

64 *occurrence), you can always pick up something wonderful in the shops onboard the ship or in a port of call.*

Don't overpack, don't overpack, don't overpack! Think in terms of essentials. Save room for the stuff you'll be buying (inevitably) on your trip.

When taking a seven-day cruise, don't pack more than one piece of luggage and one carry-on bag. Less is better.

Be aware that the airlines are enforcing their carry-on luggage policy, so be sure your cruise agent has provided information regarding the size of your bags. Again, less is always better.

Once you finalize your list of things to take, stick to it. Too often people develop a superb list, only to ignore it during the actual packing. Caught up in the heat of the moment, they start tossing things into the suitcase with abandon. Usually these items are never used on the vacation.

A good packing rule to remember when going on a
cruise: When in doubt, leave it out!

Bring an attractive cover-up that will carry you ele-
gantly from pool to cabin. In fact, when choosing all
of your wardrobe, go for classy rather than gaudy.
It won't cost any more, and you'll look better!

Bring a backpack. You can use it as carry-on luggage to and from the ship, and it will be handy both
on the ship and on shore excursions.

Pack workout gear if you plan to take advantage of
the health-club facilities onboard.

Most cruises provide a mix of casual, informal, and
formal evenings. Ask your cruise agent to find out
from the cruise line what mix your voyage will offer
so you can plan your wardrobe accordingly.

While most cruise ships offer dry cleaning, opt for
washable items whenever possible. Who needs the
hassle and expense of dry cleaning on vacation?

66   People often get carried away when it comes to shoes, which take up a lot of luggage space. Try to bring just one pair of walking shoes, one pair of versatile casual shoes, and one pair of dressy shoes. (You certainly know a cruise is not the time to break in a new pair of shoes.)

Pack some moisturized wipes. They will always come in handy, especially when cruising with children and while on shore excursions.

Because of the variety of food offered onboard the ship and in the ports, you may be tempted to try different types of spicy foods for the first time. Pack an antacid, just in case!

A cruise is a great place to show off jewelry, especially on formal evenings, but don't bring anything that you could not bear losing, such as family heirlooms. Cubic zirconia is the way to go.

On a cruise, women can get a lot of use out of leggings. Not only can they be dressed up or down very easily, but they can also be hand-washed.

If you really *must* bring work with you while on your cruise and you intend to pack your laptop computer, know that most new cruise ships have Internet access in the staterooms. There is a nominal fee and every ship and cruise line is different. Be sure you've packed your laptop in your carry-on bag so it is accessible for airport and pier authorities to check.

Bring a night light to place in the bathroom or a small flashlight for use in the middle of the night. This will be especially useful for passengers with inside cabins.

If you are traveling with a child who wets the bed, pack a plastic sheet to protect the ship's berth.

Carry some business cards. You never know what kind of contacts you will make among your fellow passengers.

68 Pack a small pair of binoculars, especially if you are cruising to an area where you will be looking at wildlife.

If you wear glasses or contact lenses or take prescription medicine, pack extras in your carry-on bags.

Pack clothing with elastic waistbands. You will feel more comfortable at the end of the cruise, when it is likely you will have gained a pound or two . . . or five!

Don't bring more than a couple of T-shirts. You will probably buy some in the ports of call or in the shops onboard the ship.

Surely you won't forget to bring sunblock or sunscreen!

Toss in a highlighter marker so you can easily mark the activities on the daily program that interest you.

Pack a small first-aid kit to take with you on your shore excursions. This will help if you have a minor injury and do not want to pay for treatment at the medical facility onboard the ship.

Bring insect repellent if mosquitoes or other pesky insects lurk in the ports of call you will be visiting or if you are sailing on a river cruise.

If you will be cruising in an area that is warm or hot, pack lightweight, loose-fitting clothes that can be easily washed and dried.

If you will be visiting an area that is cold, pack a warm coat with a lining that can be easily removed.

If you are cruising in an area where the local residents speak a foreign language, pack a small phrase book and memorize some key phrases.

Men will find nylon swim shorts with pockets to be

very versatile. They can be used as walking shorts, and they dry quickly.

Pack toiletries, prescriptions, and other things you can't do without, plus a change of clothing, in one of your carry-on bags. In the event your check-in luggage is lost or stolen and does not arrive at the ship, you will have some essentials to keep you fresh for a couple of days.

Pack a copy of your living will. Unfortunately, a cruise vacation is not immune to fatal circumstances.

Bring an umbrella to protect you from rain, snow, or sun.

Pack a hat, pack a hat, pack a hat!

Invest in a good pair of sunglasses. Even in frigid regions, the glare from the sun can be intense onboard.

Even though most cruise ships provide a wake-up service, pack a battery-run alarm clock. (P.S. Don't forget extra batteries.)

Although every effort is made to keep you comfortable inside the ship, the air-conditioning can get too cool in some of the public lounges. Pack a sweater or jacket, preferably versatile enough in style to carry you from day to night.

When flying from a very cold climate to a very warm point of embarkation, pack your coat in your luggage just before you check it in with the airline agent.

I have to say it again: Don't overpack!

HOW TO PACK

Packing well may be an art form, but there's nothing mysterious about it. These tips will help you organize your belongings to minimize clutter and wrinkling and to allow for easy "loading" and "offloading" both before and after your trip.

72 Pack your liquid toiletry items in sealable plastic bags, and place these bags in another sealed plastic container. This is double protection against damaging your clothing or other items in your suitcase. Also make sure these containers are not filled to the top.

Place the heaviest items on the bottom of your suitcase and the lighter items on top.

Protect your clothing from shoe polish by slipping each of your shoes into an old sock or a plastic bag.

Fold shirts and blouses by making the crease below the waistline. This will help prevent wrinkle lines across the areas that show.

Packing light is the best revenge. If you can manage to pack all your belongings into two carry-on bags, you will save time and not risk having your luggage tampered with or lost. It might be wise, however, to have your cruise agent check with the airline to see how many carry-on bags are allowed per passenger.

When you are cruising to a place that will require you to wear a heavy coat, don't pack it, carry it instead. This is also true for boots, heavy sweaters, or anything bulky that will take up a lot of room in your suitcase.

Expandable luggage will prove to be beneficial when you are bringing home the souvenirs you bought during your cruise.

Tie a closed identification tag with your name, cruise line and ship, and address and phone number (preferably those of your business, for security's sake) to the handle of each piece of luggage, including your carry-on bags.

As an additional means of identification, tape the above information to the inside of each piece of luggage in case the outside luggage tag gets torn off.

74   In most cases, you will be directed or personally escorted to your cabin when you embark on the ship. Your luggage may not arrive for two or three hours. Don't panic. The crew members on the ship have nearly 4,000 pieces to sort and distribute—it takes time. If the ship is ready to sail and you have not yet received your bags, contact the purser's desk or the housekeeping department to ask for assistance.

If your luggage gets lost, don't let it ruin your cruise. You can purchase what you need in the onboard gift shop or in the first port of call. (Of course, you already know that irreplaceable items such as prescription medicine and all valuables should be packed in your carry-on bags.)

Do not lock your luggage with small locks or with the combination that might be on your bags. For security reasons, all luggage must be available and easy to open for inspection.

If your air transportation is *not* part of the cruise package, you will have to collect your own luggage in the baggage claim area before transferring to the ship.

❄

In the event your luggage does not arrive at the ship and the cruise line and airline are unable to find it, you may be entitled to an "onboard credit" for up to $100 in the ship's gift shop. This will allow you to buy toiletries and a few items of clothing to help you get by until the luggage is found. Contact the information desk onboard the ship for assistance. If you purchased travel insurance, you may be compensated.

❄

Don't overpack! (I had to mention it again, just in case you hadn't gotten the message yet.)

TRAVEL DOCUMENTS

It's the packet of information that makes your adrenaline flow: your cruise documents. These papers are your ticket to an exciting adventure. Your cruise agent will receive them a couple of weeks before your departure date and will make sure they are in order before mailing them or

76 *calling you to pick them up. Keep these documents in a safe place, and once you are onboard the ship, lock them in the safe in your cabin.*

You are not allowed to use a passport as your proof of citizenship if it is due to expire within six months of embarking on your cruise.

Never pack cash, traveler's checks, travel documents, prescription medicine, or other valuable items in your check-in luggage. Keep these with you in a secure carry-on bag.

Proper identification and proof of citizenship are mandatory to board the cruise ship. If you fail to provide this to the cruise line's embarkation staff, you will not, under any circumstances, be allowed to board the ship and no refund will be given to you. A valid passport or certified copy of your birth certificate is needed.

Make two photocopies of your passport, driver's license, medical insurance card, prescriptions, airline tickets, cruise agent's name and telephone number, credit-card numbers, and any other important information. Leave one copy with a family member and keep one copy of these documents with you in a safe place while you are traveling, such as in the safe in your cabin.

When cruising abroad, ask your cruise agent (at least six months in advance) if you will need a vaccination or medical certificate. Some countries require these, and you do not want to leave such things to the last minute.

Your cruise agent will let you know if you will need a passport to enter any ports of call. Obtaining a passport is easy and inexpensive. Call the United States Passport Agency to obtain information (its twenty-four-hour phone number is 202–647–0518). You can also call your local courthouse or post office for information.

NAVIGATING AIR-SEA TRANSFERS

Your house is locked up tight, mail and newspaper delivery has been stopped, and Rover has

78 *been left in the neighbor's care. Finally, you're ready to leave on your big adventure!*

But before you can begin cruising, you may have to fly to the embarkation point. While it's true that transfers between airports and cruise-line terminals can be tedious, a few tips should help ease the pain.

Connecting flights have a way of making people tired. Opt for nonstop flights to your embarkation port whenever possible, even if it costs a bit more.

If your flight to meet the ship is long, wear casual clothes on the plane. Take off your shoes and put on a thick pair of socks. You'll feel much better and arrive in better spirits.

When cruising during big holidays, arrive at the airport at least three hours before your scheduled flight. Airlines do occasionally overbook, the people who check in first have priority, and latecomers will be bumped. You don't want this to happen to you—unless, of course, you're hoping to get bumped in return for a free-flight coupon. Be sure there's enough time before your cruise begins to catch another flight.

Have your cruise agent book an early enough flight so that you will not panic about missing the ship. It is advisable to fly a day prior to embarking onto the ship. When you get off the airplane, you will be greeted by a cruise-line representative, either at the gate or in the baggage claim area. The representative will tell you what to do and where to go from there.

If you've purchased a hotel package with the cruise line, ask your cruise agent to confirm there will be ground transportation from the airport to the hotel and to the ship the following day. Be sure you have transfer coupons for this.

Take special care in transferring your luggage in and out of taxis and hotels, prior to embarking onto the ship. Be sure you have every piece of luggage with you before you leave these places.

80 If for any reason you happen to miss the ship, contact the cruise line's port agent at the pier. They might be able to help you with a charter boat or tug to get you to your ship. Otherwise, they'll help arrange air transportation to the ship's next port of call. (This emergency transportation will be at your expense.)

For security reasons, passengers are never allowed to bring visitors onboard the ship, even on the day of embarkation.

If you fly to another country to meet the ship, you will be required to collect your luggage and pass through customs. At that point you will be instructed by the cruise-line representative on where to proceed.

EMBARKATION AT LAST!

Embarkation. Even the sound of the word generates excitement and fun. It's the start of your long-awaited vacation as you walk up the gang-

way to go onboard the ship. Not only are you embarking onto the ship, you are embarking on a new adventure. Have fun!

Embarkation is a very busy time for the staff and crew members. When checking in at the cruise-ship terminal, have all your cruise documents filled out and ready to hand to the staff. This will help speed up the embarkation process immensely.

If you are a frequent cruiser and belong to a cruise line's repeat-passenger club, there is usually a separate check-in place for you and everyone in your party. Sometimes these lines are longer because there are so many repeat passengers. Play it by ear.

After your cruise documents have been checked, you will be told where to go to walk onto the ship. There is usually a photographer standing at the entrance of the ship, ready to snap a picture of you with your windblown hair, faded makeup, wrinkled clothing, and exhausted smile. Don't worry—you can use that photograph as your "before" cruise picture.

82 If the ship's crew members escort you to your cabin, give them a tip. Just like hotel employees, these ladies and gentlemen are accustomed to receiving a couple of dollars for their service.

Once you have unpacked your clothing, get a small map of the ship from a crew member and start exploring.

As soon as you get onboard, your cruise experience begins in a most welcome way: You will be offered a buffet meal, usually in the cafe on the top deck.

YOUR MONEY

Going on a cruise could be the best investment you'll ever make in your life. What you will learn in one week on a cruise is often greater than the education you would get for a semester at college. To get a full return on your investment, know how to handle your money while cruisin'.

Your onboard cruise card is activated by using a major credit card. This card is also used for identification when you leave and board the ship and sometimes as the key to your stateroom. Don't for-get—as with any charge card, this bill has to be paid! If you are on a budget, check your balance daily to monitor how much you are spending.

Personal checks are rarely accepted onboard a ship, so be sure you have enough cash or credit on your personal credit card to pay for your onboard purchases. Many cruise lines have ATM machines onboard (usually found near the casino) in the event you need extra cash.

Use a credit card instead of cash whenever possi-ble. Although the bill will make your throat seize up momentarily, you'll soon realize that this approach usually provides a better exchange rate than a bank or airport booth.

If you are cruising in a foreign country, cruise lines will often arrange for the local bank authorities to exchange currency onboard the ship.

84   U.S. currency is accepted in many ports of call. Ask the purser's staff for guidance in this area.

At the end of your cruise, you will receive an itemized statement for all your onboard purchases. After you check it over to make sure everything is correct, your charges will automatically be transferred to the credit card you used to activate your cruise card. You will not have to wait in a long line on the final night to pay your bill.

If you disagree with anything on your bill, discuss it with the purser's staff on the final night or the final morning.

Before making a telephone call from the ship, find out how much it will cost. Sometimes a call may cost up to $15 per minute! Thus, if you need to reach someone at home, wait until the ship docks in port and call from a pay telephone. If you do not have a calling card, in many cases there will be a calling booth nearby where you can buy one.

On some ships you can make calls from your own cellular phone. If it's that important for you to be easily accessible by phone, ask your local cellular dealer for details about cell phones with a "roam" feature.

When using a calling card at a pay phone that has a push-button system and you want to make more than one call, don't hang up the telephone when you have completed your call. If you press the # (pound) key after the other party has hung up, you will get another dial tone and won't be charged an additional connection fee.

SETTLING IN

WHILE EACH SHIP AND EACH CRUISE are unique, there are certain commonalities in the world of cruising. Knowing what to expect onboard from the cruise staff and crew—and knowing what is expected of you and your fellow passengers—will enrich your vacation and the relationships you form onboard.

THE STAFF AND CREW

Most of the staff and crew are genuinely happy to have you onboard the ship, whether it's a luxury liner or a freighter. They are well trained in their jobs, and they are often very interesting people. You'll have no problem making friends among them, and you'll be glad you did.

Just ask! This is one of the best tips in the entire book. You will be amazed at how much the staff and crew of cruise ships are willing to accommodate your needs.

88   If you have a waiter, busboy, or cabin steward who tells you he may get fired from the cruise line unless you give him an "excellent" rating on the comment cards, report this to the hotel manager onboard the ship. This is not true, and the cruise lines will not tolerate this type of behavior.

Don't ask the captain "Who's drivin' the boat?" when you greet him at the welcome-aboard cocktail party. Spare him—he's heard this line a thousand times.

The ship is your home away from home for a week or so. However, it is home for the crew members and staff for much longer periods. Respect the signs that say CREW ONLY. These areas are the only places they have for privacy and to take their minds off work. Think of it this way: Would you want your customers and clients pushing their way into your living room?

The cruise staff are the fun people onboard the ship, or they should be. Whenever they are involved in an activity or event, you can expect a good time.

If they ask for a volunteer to help them out, do it! You'll be glad you did.

At the end of the cruise, you will be asked to fill out a comment card. If you received particularly good service from any staff members, be sure to note their names. This is how many employees on cruise ships get their promotions and raises.

If you are going to criticize something or someone on the comment card, suggest how the problem might be solved. Cruise lines are more receptive to complaints if they are accompanied by a solution.

Get to know the staff early in the cruise. They can give you some wonderful inside information regarding the ports of call, excursions, activities, and so on.

The social hostess or concierge is usually responsible for selecting guests to sit at the captain's table for dinner. Talk with either of them if you are interested in having dinner with the captain. Usually VIPs, celebrities, passengers in the owners'

90   suite, frequent travelers with the cruise line, or people who present themselves as sophisticated and fun are selected for this. Sometimes passengers who have experienced an unfortunate mishap on the ship will be invited in order to smooth things over.

It is possible that you are not accustomed to having maid service or cabin service as is provided on the ship. Do not let this intimidate you and don't be rude or excessively demanding. These are respectable jobs that require long hours. Be respectful and appreciative of these employees.

There are times when cruise agents have promised that the ship will provide something but, due to circumstances beyond their control, the ship's staff and crew are unable to deliver. For example, the Jacuzzi in your suite may expire halfway through the cruise and the part to fix it won't be available for a week or so. Unless it is a matter of life or death, let it go. Don't allow it to upset you.

TIPPING GUIDELINES

One of the questions I'm most often asked about cruising is proper tipping etiquette. It is an issue that creates a great deal of anxiety among cruisers, but a few simple guidelines will help you navigate these particular waters. Please follow the suggestions provided here and by your cruise line. What you leave these people as your gratuity for the week is important, not a favor. Be a good tipper.

Some cruise lines include tipping in the price of the cruise fare; others do not. If gratuities are not included in the fare, give what is recommended by the cruise line directly to the individuals who are supposed to receive the tip. Cruise lines will provide special tip envelopes near the end of your cruise.

If the cruise is longer than two weeks, it is customary to tip a portion of the gratuity midway through the voyage and the remainder on the last evening.

92 Some cruise lines demand prepaid gratuities. If this is the case, have this amount taken off your account on the first day of the cruise and tell the guest relations staff you will be paying the gratuities yourself at the end of the cruise. This assures that the staff will provide the best possible service the entire cruise *(and be sure you are generous with your tips when they do).*

The average amount of money for tips for a passenger on a one-week cruise is approximately $75—not a bad deal at all for the fabulous service provided.

It is not necessary to tip the head of a department, like the cruise director, hotel manager, purser, bar manager, chief cabin steward, or executive chef. These people make great salaries and do not expect any extra compensation for doing their job well. Buy them a drink and toast their professional talent.

Take a moment at the end of your cruise to write

thank-you notes to members of the crew and staff who have really made a difference in the success of your vacation. Written words of appreciation are sometimes just as important as the cash tip.

A 15 percent tip is automatically added to the check for most of the drinks and bottles of wine that you order in the lounges. If you have been a regular customer to a particular bartender, however, leave that person some extra money on the last day of the cruise.

WHAT TO DO IF THERE IS A PROBLEM

Yes, problems can arise even on a luxurious cruise ship. If they do, take a deep breath—and then get over it! Life is too short to get stressed out about whether someone has cut in front of you while you were standing in line at the midnight buffet or whether you won that imitation-leather key ring at shuffleboard. And if the only problem you run into is the fact that your clothing has inexplicably shrunk by the end of the cruise, consider yourself a contented cruiser!

94   If there is a problem, gather all the facts before talking with the staff, and don't raise your voice or get hostile. If possible, back up your complaint with documentation or witnesses. If you present yourself as being civilized and level-headed, your complaint will be taken seriously. People who act like hotheads or hysterics will be viewed more skeptically.

Cruise lines are always anxious to settle disputes with unhappy passengers, providing the complaint is reasonable. The last thing a cruise company wants is bad publicity.

The staff and crew want to do everything possible to see that you have a wonderful cruise. Don't hold in your complaint until the last day, and then "let 'em have it" in the comment cards. If you do that, you'll probably have built up some resentment. Speak up early!

Present any complaint to the manager of the department where the problem occurred.

Should you encounter a problem with your cabin—
for example, there is excessive noise from the gen-
erators, the category of the cabin is not what you
paid for, the plumbing is not working correctly—
contact the hotel manager immediately and ask to
be moved to another cabin. If there are no other
cabins available, ask the manager to give you written confirmation acknowledging that these problems do exist. When presented in a fair way, the
cruise line may issue you a partial refund. Be sure
that your cruise agent follows up on this.

Most types of legal action brought against a cruise
line will be heard in a federal court, as all cruise
ships operate under maritime law. But this is an
ordeal; try to settle any disputes out of court.

If you cannot reach an agreement with a cruise line
and feel that your only alternative is to seek legal
action, you must act within the deadline specified
in your cruise contract. If you don't, you could for-
feit your right to any case whatsoever.

If your cruise agent made arrangements with the

96   cruise line's corporate office regarding something special for you onboard the ship, and for some reason it has not come about, talk to the hotel manager's staff. Sometimes inexperienced cruise agents promise things that are impossible for the ship's staff to accommodate. Occasionally, the information from the cruise agent to the office to the ship gets lost. Be patient with the onboard personnel until the problem is solved.

CRUISE ETIQUETTE

In the years that I have been cruising, I have witnessed some really remarkable things, both good and bad. Can you imagine two eighty-year-old ladies fistfighting because they wanted to dance with the same dance host at the same time? Or passengers sitting in their cabin on the last night of the cruise ordering room service so they didn't have to tip their waiter and busboy in the dining room? Although some of these tips may be simple, common-sense suggestions, they serve as a reminder for those who need to brush up on their etiquette.

Don't expect everything to be perfect on your cruise! Brace yourself; it is not going to be, even if you have spent thousands of dollars. You may encounter rough weather, a water pipe may break in your cabin, your dining-table mates might be miserable human beings. No matter what happens, go with the float—I mean flow. Have a good cruise attitude!

Laundry can pile up on a cruise, especially if there are children along. Some ships have a laundry facility on each deck. If the ship you are traveling on does not have a laundry facility and you do not want to pay to have your clothes cleaned, fill the sink in your cabin with water and add a dash of shampoo. Hang the clothes to dry on the clothesline above the shower—not draped all over the furniture.

Most cruise ships offer a selection of books in the library. If you check one out during the cruise, be sure to return it before disembarkation. (If you take it home, you may be charged.)

98 Use the right nautical terminology. The ship is called a ship—not a boat. And the port side of the ship is on the left and the starboard side is on the right. (It is easy to remember this because *port* and *left* both have four letters.) The front of the ship, or pointy end, is called the bow; the blunt end is the aft.

Elevators will be crowded around mealtimes, before and after the evening shows, and on the morning when passengers are leaving the ship. To help ease the crunch, head for the stairs during those times, if possible.

To mail postcards and letters from the ship, take them to the reception desk. The receptionist will have them posted in the next port of call. In most cases, of course, you will have to pay the postage.

There should be complimentary stationery and postcards in your cabin. If you do not find any, contact the information or reception desk.

When leaving your cabin, don't slam the door. Others who are staying in the cabins near yours may be sleeping or resting. Show the same consideration that you would like to receive from them.

The ship is your home for the duration of the cruise, but that doesn't mean normal civilities can be dropped. Be polite and pleasant to those around you.

Keep a grip on yourself. Getting a little tipsy and kicking up your heels on the dance floor is one thing; reeling around knocking over tables in the bar or starting an ugly argument is quite another. If you make a fool or pest of yourself because you have had too much to drink, you'll have to face the witnesses in the morning. You don't want to spend your vacation slinking around the ship, trying to avoid those people.

Be discreet with your money and personal wealth. Nobody really cares, and being ostentatious is in bad taste.

100 The ship is indeed your home away from home, but it's still a public facility. Don't wander around outside your cabin in nightie and curlers.

In the same vein, please be modest in your attire. It's not necessary for every person on the ship to become acquainted with your every bulge and curve.

Don't walk around the inside of the ship in a bathing suit without a cover-up.

If there is a long line to greet the captain at the welcome-aboard cocktail party, relax in one of the lounges until the line tapers off. You can then walk in as an individual and not as part of the herd!

To be asked to dine with the captain is an honor. Don't ever decline.

Don't drape your belongings over the deck chairs

to reserve them for later. These chairs are for everyone. Unless you are ready to use them, leave them for someone else.

Don't sit in the front row of an evening show if you are tired and could easily fall asleep after a long day of sightseeing. Others may be distracted by watching your head bob up and down. And the entertainers certainly don't want to look out and see people dozing during their act.

If you are on a cruise where the announcements are translated into three or four different languages, be patient. Sometimes the information concerns safety matters, and it is important that all the passengers understand the procedures.

If you are cruising with another person or group of people, be a good cruise companion. Don't complain or grumble about things. It will not only bring negative energy to your vacation, but you will embarrass the people with you and around you. If there's a problem, handle it quietly and privately

102 with the cruise staff and crew; don't bore your fellow passengers with it.

Give your cabin mate some space so that you don't get on each other's nerves. Agree to participate in a few activities separately, and establish other ground rules before you embark on the cruise.

There is a reason why cruise ships do not sell gum onboard the ship. Parents, make sure your children dispose of their gum in the garbage container and not on or under the furniture.

If you have been trekking through a muddy rain forest during a tour, be considerate and do not track the mud through the ship. Take off your shoes or boots before entering the ship and carry them with you to your cabin. Once you get to your cabin, you can wash them off in the shower.

Sit at least ten rows back from the stage if you are bringing small children to the shows. If they start getting restless and talking, it will be less distract-

ing to the rest of the audience and the performers 103
on stage.

If the sun shines, smile. If it rains, smile and look for
the rainbow.

Take a moment to commend any of the staff and
crew members you feel are doing a great job. A pat
on the back goes a long way.

CRUISIN'

DRAWING FROM MY ONBOARD EXPERIENCES with now over one million people, I think I know the secret to having a really great cruise. The passengers who seem to have an absolute blast are those who have a great attitude. These people roll with the punches, are not afraid to participate in the activities, and somehow open their minds and hearts to the cruise adventure. They are nonjudgmental, a quality that allows them to be free spirits onboard the ship. Thus, to make the most of your cruise, follow this motto: Participate, don't anticipate.

BON APPETIT!

One phrase is used over and over again onboard a cruise ship: "Maybe I'll have just one more slice." Everything you have heard about the food on a cruise ship is true: It is wonderful. Don't even think about dieting while onboard the ship!

Have a healthy portion of Baked Alaska. It is part of cruising tradition.

106 Since meals in the main dining room are included in the cost, a cruise ship is a good place to try different kinds of foods. Be adventurous—you might fall in love with an entirely new kind of cuisine.

If your cruise ship offers specialty dining rooms, make your reservations on the first day of the cruise and ask for a table next to the window. These restaurants may have a surcharge, but they will be worth the money you pay.

Cruise ships will provide special meals for those on salt-free, sugar-free, low-fat, or diabetic diets. Your cruise agent can arrange this for you in advance, or you can make arrangements with the maitre d' once you are onboard.

By all means indulge in the midnight buffet, but take a small plate. You'll be able to sample everything, but in smaller portions. You'll sleep better for it!

A good way to placate a bulging stomach is to take a stroll on the outside deck after each meal.

Very often, table mates in the dining room start the cruise as strangers and finish as good, lifelong friends. But if you sense a personality clash early on, don't hesitate—be pleasant during the meal, and later on discreetly arrange with the headwaiter or the maitre d' to be moved to another table.

If you have had a great time with your table mates, surprise everyone with a nice bottle of champagne on the last night of the cruise and toast to a future reunion.

Cruise ships often have "open sitting" lunches. These give you an opportunity to sit with passengers other than your usual dinner companions. It's another great way to meet fellow cruisers.

Try not to eat more than five meals a day!

Don't complain at your dinner table. It will bring everyone down.

When you arrive onboard, you will need to confirm

108   your dining room reservations. If the ship has two separate seatings and space is not available on the one you requested, contact the maitre d'. Sometimes a $10 tip will find you in the right time and place!

The barrage of cutlery at the dinner table may look overwhelming when you sit down to eat. Basically, the rule is to start with the outside silverware and work your way toward the plate as the courses progress. (Some ships offer a table-etiquette class for those who are really concerned about the proper use of silverware and table manners. This is not offered to insult anyone.)

Many of the larger ships offer pizzerias and other venues for casual dining. These places are more desirable when traveling with children or if you want a change from the formalities of the dining room. It is also a lot quicker.

Tables in the dining room are designed to accommodate two, four, six, eight, or ten people. If you are a large group or family, ask the maitre d' if you can be seated at adjoining tables.

Some cabins have a minibar. Just like in hotels, there is a charge for anything you eat or drink from it unless you are in a suite. All those traveling with you should be warned about this, as the cost can be substantial.

Do not leave food lying around in your cabin. It is a continuous battle for the cruise lines to control insects onboard their ships.

If you or your children are used to eating dinner at 5:30 P.M. and the first seating for dinner is at 6:30 P.M., start adjusting mealtimes at home at least two weeks prior to the cruise.

If your cabin has a small refrigerator, you can use it to store fruit, yogurt, or other small snacks from the buffet for later in the day.

110 If your cruise line offers a choice of seatings, consider requesting the later seating. You can stay in port longer, sleep later in the morning, and participate in more of the late-evening activities—for many people, this lifestyle is a delightful change from their normal routines.

Many cruise ships offer alternative dining areas. If you do not wish to get dressed in formal attire, opt for the casual dinner buffet in the cafe upstairs.

Some cruise lines offer open-seating dining, which gives you the opportunity to dine anytime you wish and sit with whomever you would like. The only problem you might face is a long line of people wanting to eat at the same time.

HEALTH AND BEAUTY

Imagine sitting in a deck chair, soaking in the warm rays of the sun as a crew member walks around the pool area spritzing you with cool mist every fifteen minutes, or lounging in the Jacuzzi before receiving an hour-long massage. Those who have been on cruises have fond memories of the pampering they received onboard.

On some cruise ships, the health and beauty facilities are among the finest in the world. Some are more than 12,000 square feet in size! You can enjoy lifting weights, taking aerobics and yoga classes, receiving nutritional advice, and getting seaweed wraps over your entire body. The facilities offer all kinds of interesting treatments, so take advantage of their services.

Make your hair and beauty appointments early in the cruise. Even if the ship is large, the days at sea are extremely busy in this department. Massages are especially popular on cruise ships, so make an appointment early. With some cruise lines these appointments can be made a couple of weeks prior to joining the ship. Ask your cruise agent.

Some of the massage therapists have a tendency to give a very light massage. If you prefer a deep-tissue massage, tell the attendant when you make your appointment and ask for the therapist who will accommodate your request.

112 Don't scream or shout around the pool area, and don't tolerate this behavior in your children. Many people take their afternoon siesta around the pool area.

If you are interested in keeping your daily workouts going, consult with the sports instructor onboard the ship to develop your own personal program to follow during the cruise.

When you get a haircut or other beauty treatment from one of the salon attendants, proper etiquette is to tip at the end of that service, as is standard practice on land.

The gym is usually very quiet when the ship is docked in port. If you don't like a lot of people around when you're working out, consider these times.

Most swimming pools are filled with filtered salt water. Use the shower facility next to the pool to rinse yourself. Also, if you used any snorkel equipment in the pool, rinse that off as well so the salt does not damage your mask or fins.

THE CASINO

Gambling is popular on most cruise ships, and the casinos can be very glamorous. As in every casino, there is always a chance to win—and lose. It can be exciting, especially if you are one of the lucky ones cashing in a bunch of chips or yelling "Bingo!" on the last day of the cruise. Good luck!

While some ports of call have casinos, the odds of winning in them are usually poor. You'll probably have better luck on the ship.

Budget your gambling money carefully each day unless you want to find yourself washing dishes at the end of the cruise. Take only the amount of money you are willing to lose. The best odds for winning are not walking into the casino in the first place.

When gambling on the slots, try to grab the machines

114 that are positioned at the end of a row, in view of everyone. They usually pay off more frequently than the rest of the machines.

Children under eighteen years of age are not permitted to gamble in the casino.

The larger ships will have a MegaCash slot-machine area, lottery drawings, and heart-stopping bingo jackpots. Good luck!

Casino chips can be charged to your onboard credit account—but of course, at the end the cruise, you do have to pay for them!

You may get a cash advance from the casino attendants simply by presenting your onboard charge card. This amount of money will be credited to your existing account.

Ships are now so sophisticated that you can gamble right from your cabin using interactive television. Money is charged directly to your charge account, so set a limit on the amount you will spend.

ACTIVITIES AND ENTERTAINMENT

You'll never be bored on a cruise—unless you want to be. Some ships offer more than sixty activities each day! Some activities, such as art classes, are quiet and relatively solitary. Others, like organized games, are rowdy and sociable.

The great thing is, there's something for everyone. As one passenger commented, "I never thought I'd find a vacation where my husband could go and do his thing and I could do mine. It's the best vacation we've ever taken together!"

Pace yourself. Running from event to event will make you exhausted by the second day.

Take some time out to sleep in, lounge around, and kick off your shoes.

Regardless of what cabin category you have paid for, everyone has full access to the activities and events offered onboard the ship.

116 Carry a copy of the daily program so you know what time the activities are and where they are located.

Many cruise ships offer vegetable-carving and ice-carving demonstrations. People who like to cook especially enjoy these, and kids find them fascinating as well.

Some cruise ships offer a religious service daily, while others provide them only on holidays. Your cruise agent can confirm with the cruise line whether a priest, minister, or rabbi will be onboard during your cruise.

Dance classes are usually offered during the cruise. Take advantage of them, even if you do not have a partner. There's something special about dancing onboard, and there's no charge (learning on land can cost a small fortune!).

Sea air makes many people especially hungry and

sleepy. Take a power nap in the afternoon so that you have reserves of energy to enjoy all the wonderful things available in the evening.

✹

The movie theater onboard the ship will be showing the latest feature films. Sometimes this room is particularly cool, so bring a sweater or shawl.

✹

If foreign-language classes are offered, surprise your family at dinner with some of the new phrases you've learned.

✹

Ask one of the performers in the show to take you backstage and show you around. Perhaps you will be able to see the costumes and props used in the production. It is fascinating and lots of fun.

✹

Some ships hold a mock Kentucky Derby horse race. If you are traveling with your family or a group of friends, bid on a wooden horse. The winners receive a cash prize, and you'll have a great time dressing the horse, giving it a name, and cheering it down the track.

118 Be pleasant when you are participating in any competitive activities on the ship. Having fun—not winning—is what it's all about. Besides, a prize like a plastic water bottle is not worth getting upset over!

There is nothing like an early morning jog on the top deck of the ship to start your day. You may even want to participate in the walk-a-mile program organized by the staff.

Most activities are free, but a few are not. Be sure to ask the staff in advance if you will have to pay to participate. Wine tasting and some craft activities may require a nominal fee.

Cruise lines often display elaborate artwork throughout their ships. Take time out to appreciate it. Some ships offer "tours" of the works and give a brief history of the artists.

Some cruise ships offer art auctions. If you collect art—and even if you don't—stop by to see what is available. Many times the prices of these pieces are a fraction of gallery prices. (If they serve complimentary champagne at these auctions, be careful how much you drink. You may end up buying something you later wish you hadn't.)

If you love the entertainment, reward the performers with a standing ovation. It's not easy to sing and dance on a moving ship!

If you would like to sit close to the stage during the evening shows, skip dessert to arrive earlier and nab the choice seats. You can always satisfy that sweet tooth at the midnight buffet.

Most engine rooms are off-limits to passengers, but you can sign up for the galley and bridge tours. Tours will give you a good look at the behind-the-scenes operations of a cruise ship. These are especially great activities for children.

The daily program may include "Friends of Dr. Bob and Bill W." This is the code for Alcoholics Anonymous meetings. AA members should contact the cruise director if these meetings are not listed in the daily program.

120 Onboard guest lecturers can give you valuable information about finances, bridge playing, life enrichment, color enhancement, and umpteen more topics. These lectures are complimentary, so take advantage of them.

If the sound is too loud in a particular lounge or theater, you may be sitting in front of a speaker or monitor. The central part of the room is usually best for sound and sight lines. If the volume is really too loud, contact the cruise director to sort out the problem.

When performers ask for volunteers to come up on the stage and participate in the show, do it. You may feel silly at first, but it will be the first thing you talk about when you get home.

ONBOARD SHOPPING

Many ships offer a veritable cornucopia of shopping opportunities. There are clothing boutiques, fine jewelry stores, perfume salons, shops with souvenirs and sundries, and everything in between. In fact, you could probably outfit your-

self entirely onboard if you prefer to travel really light and bring along no luggage at all!

Most cruise lines provide duty-free specialty shops onboard their ships. (Duty-free means there are no taxes on the items.) Daily sales often sprout up, so stop in and see what is discounted each day.

Compare the prices of the merchandise sold onboard the ship with the same items sold in the ports of call. In most cases, you will find better prices onboard the ship.

Purchase some "logo wear" in the onboard shop. This is merchandise that has the name of the ship and cruise line on it. When you get home, all you have to do is wear it around and people will know you've been on a cruise.

If the toiletries you need are not provided in your cabin, they will probably be available in the gift shop.

Many cruise ships sell loose gemstones in one of

122 their onboard shops. Often these offer exceptional quality and value, so take advantage of this if you plan to buy jewelry.

PHOTOGRAPHERS AND PHOTOGRAPHS

Photographs are an important part of your cruise experience. Throw all caution to the wind and snap, snap, snap. Though you might cringe when you get the bill for developing your multiple rolls of film, you'll enjoy a return on the investment for the rest of your life, as you will reminisce over the pictures again and again.

There is no obligation to purchase any of the photographs taken by the photographers onboard the ship. Give them a smile wherever they may be.

If you are traveling with a group of friends or associates, make arrangements with the ship's photographer to meet everyone in a nice area of the ship. One that has a great background, such as a grand staircase or painting, is ideal. You may even consider having this picture taken in one of the ports of call. Don't forget to ask the photographer to give 123 you a good price.

Buy a disposable camera for children over five years old traveling in your family, and let them take pictures throughout the cruise. When you return home, help them make a scrapbook.

Cruise-line photographers use digital cameras on most ships today. They can place any kind of background you would like to have on your pictures. Some ships are so advanced that the photos can be downloaded from the digital camera right into the television in your cabin. You can then choose which photographs you want to order from what you see on the screen.

Buy photographs in the photo gallery of you and your special someone. At the end of the cruise, have them placed in a nice album and give it to your partner as a special gift. It will be cherished for years.

124 Bring along a good camera or video recorder; you'll be glad you did.

❄

The cruise line may provide a videographer to videotape passengers participating in various shore excursions and activities. Smile for the camera—you may just want to purchase a copy of the video before you leave the ship.

❄

If you are traveling with your family, have a family portrait taken on one of the formal evenings. Ask the photographer to have copies made for each family member. That picture will be a wonderful reminder of your family adventure on the high seas.

❄

Ask the photographer to take a photograph of everyone sitting at your dining table. Later, buy a copy for everyone and present it to them on the last night of the cruise.

❄

Purchase pictures taken by the ship's photographers that show the places and ports you have visited during your cruise. Some of these shots are better than the postcards you can buy from the local shops (and undoubtedly better than the average shutterbug's efforts).

✿

Develop at least one roll of film onboard, if not all of them. That way you will know whether your camera is working correctly and whether you need some suggestions from the ship's photographers to improve your shots.

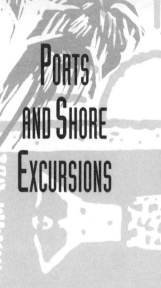

PORTS AND SHORE EXCURSIONS

ONE OF THE THINGS THAT MAKES a cruise so unique, so different from any other vacation, is the opportunity to explore different ports of call and to go on a wide variety of shore excursions. There are, of course, tours of these ports, by foot, car, or bus; and shopping is always fun in a new place.

Some of my fondest memories of cruises are linked to special land excursions. Imagine going on a safari in Africa, riding in a helicopter over a volcano in Hawaii, floating in a dugout canoe down the Amazon River, walking on the Great Wall of China, holding a koala in Australia, walking among the penguins in Antarctica, or traversing a glacier in Alaska. Such exciting adventures are available to passengers at an additional cost, but they are wonderful memories that will last a lifetime.

PLANNING AHEAD

Because your time is limited in each port of call, it is important to do some research and plan ahead.

128 *Don't be afraid to ask your cruise agent a hundred questions, and check the Internet for additional information. What you learn can make a huge difference in the quality of your vacation.*

Before leaving on the cruise, search through travel books and magazines to learn of any special festivals or holidays in the ports of call you'll be visiting.

Each country's embassy and tourism offices can provide you with valuable information about the ports of call. You can get their phone numbers by calling the information operator in most major cities.

Be sure you've booked your shore excursions in advance through the cruise line's Web site. This will ensure you'll be able to participate, even if they are sold out when you arrive onboard the ship. Ask your cruise agent to give you your booking number, as you will need this to prebook these tours.

Some cruise lines offer a private club in the ports of call. These provide a great oasis when you are out shopping and need a relaxing place to sit and have a drink. Ask your shore excursion staff if the cruise line has such a club.

The newer cruise ships are designed so that you can book your shore excursions right from your own cabin, using the remote control device. You'll find operating instructions in your cabin.

When was the last time you were on a picnic? Ask the executive chef or maitre d' to organize a picnic basket for you and your companions. You'll be amazed at how relaxing and enjoyable a simple picnic in the park can be in a new port of call.

Sometimes a cruise ship is unable to dock in a particular port and the passengers are taken ashore in tender boats. The tendering operation is explained in the daily program, and most of the time the cruise director will make an announcement

130 the night before. Be patient during the tender operations. Wait in one of the public lounges until you hear an announcement for your group to proceed to the gangway and go ashore. Passengers booked on a shore excursion are usually taken first.

It is very exciting to be outside when the ship is approaching or leaving any port of call. Walk around and take in the view.

Sometimes it is fun to stay onboard the ship when it is docked in port. The ship has an entirely different feeling when most of the passengers have left.

Be a good traveler: Learn a few key phrases—like "Please" and "Thank you"—in the language of each country you'll be visiting.

If you are returning to a port of call that you have

visited in the past, don't expect everything to be the same. Explore with an open mind.

Find out as many details about the shore excursions as you can. If the staff doesn't have the answers, ask them to find out for you. This will help prevent unpleasant surprises, such as going on an excursion that involves a half-mile hike up to a waterfall—when you twisted your ankle two days before.

Many island ports of call have beautiful resort hotels. Consider spending the day enjoying the facilities at one of these places. In most cases, the managers of these resorts welcome cruise-ship passengers, because they know they will be spending money on food, drinks, and souvenirs. They also hope that you'll return at a later date and stay at the hotel.

Some items sold in the more exotic ports of call are not allowed to be brought into your home country.

132 Check with the shore excursion staff or port lecturer to learn if any items in the port of call are included on this list.

Before going into port, check the time that you must be back onboard. (Usually it is thirty minutes before sailing time.) If you miss the ship, you will be responsible for getting yourself to the next port of call to rejoin the cruise—a very expensive mistake!

In some cases, cruise lines are not legally responsible for shore excursions; the tour operators they use for excursions may be independent contractors, thereby releasing the cruise lines of any liability. If you have an accident or mishap during an organized shore excursion, the cruise lines may help, but they are not legally obligated. Make sure that your insurance covers you for situations like this.

Ask the shore excursion staff about the tipping policy in the ports you will be visiting. For example, in many places, tips for waiters are included in the restaurant check.

Be aware that people may badger you for hand-outs as you walk around some ports and tourist spots. If this would bother you excessively, you will probably be happier taking a guided bus or taxi tour of the port of call.

❁

If you need to cancel a tour or shore excursion because of an illness, contact the tour office as soon as you can. In most cases, your money will be refunded, provided you have a legitimate excuse and a note from the ship's doctor.

❁

Try to get the name and telephone number of the port agent, the number of the pier that the ship is docked at, and any other information that will help you remember the location of the ship. You don't want to find yourself on the other side of the island with no idea how to return to the ship.

SHOPPING!

The expression "Shop 'til you drop" is never so true as when you are on a cruise—the gift shops onboard the ship, the wide variety of retail shops

134 *in the ports of call, the vendors on the streets selling artifacts and souvenirs! Following these tips will help your shopping budget stretch further.*

If the cruise line provides one, use the recommended shopping map. If anything should break or stop working when you get home, you'll have a guarantee from the cruise line that the store will replace it. (The cruise lines receive a commission from every purchase their passengers make.)

Some ports are terrible tourist traps. Ask crew members where the real bargain places are in town.

It is easy to get caught up in the excitement of an exotic port of call. To avoid throwing your money away, follow this rule: Don't purchase anything unless you first say to yourself, "If I were walking down the street back home and saw this in the window, would I buy it?" More times than not, the answer will be no.

Before you start to buy things in the first shop you

see, look around and find out what the prices are
in some of the other shops. You'll be very upset if
you find out the bag you paid $70 for was only $50
at the store down the street.

In many parts of the world, bargaining is a form of
shopping etiquette, especially in street markets
and kiosks. In these situations, never accept the
first price offered. Make a counteroffer of less than
half what the vendors ask, and go from there to the
price you are willing to pay.

Have fun while you are bargaining. This isn't life or
death! The haggling should remain a friendly
exchange. If the vendor (or you) gets too pushy or
heated, it's time to leave.

While it's nice to get a good deal, be reasonable,
and remember that people in many ports of call are
extremely poor. Trying to chisel another dollar off
the cost of a straw hat may mean that the vendor
won't have dinner that night, while it's just pocket
change to you.

136 Street vendors who follow you around pestering you to purchase their merchandise can best be handled with a firm "No." Avoid answering their questions and looking at them or what they are carrying.

When you walk into a shop, don't go directly to the item you want to buy or make a comment about how beautiful it is. This gives the merchant too much leverage in negotiating the price.

If you want to buy several items in one store, ask the manager to make a deal, such as 10 percent off everything.

In the more exotic ports, it is common for shop owners to give a very good deal on merchandise early in the morning. (They feel that the first sale is the most important of the day.)

When bargaining, once you decide on the price you want to pay, don't go higher. If the merchant does not accept your offer, begin to walk away. Often he will call you back and sell the merchandise at the 137 price you quoted.

Avoid being ostentatious with your personal wealth. Do not wear expensive clothing and jewelry, and don't flash your cash around. Be discreet, not just to avoid being charged higher prices, but also to deter thieves.

Be aware: There is a tendency for shop owners to raise their prices when a cruise ship arrives in port. Always ask for a discount on the stated price.

Carry a small calculator to help you convert the exchange rate in foreign ports.

Buy a small piece of artwork from one of the local street vendors. For a low price, you'll have something unique that will serve as a wonderful memento back home.

In some places you can get great bargains toward the end of the tourist or cruising season.

138 When you buy something that will be shipped to your home, make sure that it is packed and the box is sealed and addressed before you leave the store. You don't want it to arrive a couple of weeks later and find that a different item has been sent, either on purpose or by mistake. Always pay with a credit card when you make purchases of this sort in case there is a dispute.

When making purchases in foreign countries using a credit card, ask the sales clerk what the rate of exchange is for that day and record it. Keep your sales receipt and compare it to your monthly credit-card statement to ensure that you have not been charged more. If there is a discrepancy, call the credit-card company to have them investigate the purchase. Avoiding this sort of problem is another reason for using the shops endorsed by the cruise line.

SIGHTSEEING AND TOURING

Face it: You're going to act like a typical tourist when you go off on your sightseeing tours. A camera will be hanging around your neck, you'll be wearing Bermuda shorts or a muu-muu and peering out from under a hat, and you'll be asking some of the same silly questions the group before asked. Even if you prefer to think of yourself as a sophisticated traveler and dress in the local garb, the people who live in the ports of call are going to take one look at you and think "tourist." Remember that everyone is a tourist outside their own country, so relax and enjoy the experience!

Treat yourself and your family to an unusual shore excursion—a helicopter ride, a submarine tour, or even a swim with the stingrays.

Everyone should snorkel at least once in their life. Give it a go!

Be polite to the people who live in the places you're visiting. While it's true that some may be trying to get you to buy something from them or to give them some money, other people may simply be

140 curious about you, in the nicest possible way. Give them the benefit of the doubt.

Don't be an obnoxious foreigner. Remember that you are the guest and that the port of call is someone else's home—not your personal playground. Be respectful of the values and mores of the country.

Small children, and even most teenagers, are not particularly fond of cathedrals and museums unless it is a very quick tour. Remember this when planning your time ashore.

Use the rest room before leaving the ship. You never know when Mother Nature will call or how long it will be before you find a facility in port—or what shape it will be in!

If you have a bus driver and tour guide on your excursion, proper etiquette is to tip each person a couple of dollars when the tour is complete.

Don't wear beachwear in port—except on the beach. Would you wear a bikini or short-shorts while strolling down Main Street in your hometown?

Ancient ruins, wineries, and old cemeteries can get boring after a couple of hours, especially if the sun is extremely hot. Remember this when you are scheduling your excursions—don't try to pack too much in, especially in the afternoon.

Most city or island tours are two to three hours in length and consist of a bus ride, some shopping, and perhaps a snack. They are a great way to become familiar with the area.

When riding on a tour bus, try to sit in the front section so you can see more easily and have a smoother ride.

If for some reason you were not happy with your shore excursion, talk (politely!) with the shore

142 excursion manager. If your complaint is fair, you may be issued a partial refund or full credit.

Carry a small bottle of water with you in case you become thirsty. But don't drink too much, unless there is a rest room nearby.

Carry some fruit in a sealable plastic bag for the kids (they always get the munchies.) And have napkins handy to clean up any mess.

If you decide to hire a taxi for the entire day in port, you can save money if you have another couple or family ride with you. This will not only give you the opportunity to make friends with some fellow passengers, but it will also be a safer ride.

When visiting cathedrals and churches, respect the environment and keep your voice low.

Children love fish and animals. A visit to an aquarium, underwater sightseeing exhibit, wildlife park, or even a submarine ride will be a big hit.

The early morning hours offer more opportunities 143 to see and photograph wildlife.

Collect a postcard from each port of call and make notes on the back, recalling your experience there.

If you or your traveling companions are adventurous cruisers, when the ship docks, contact the information center in the port of call for suggestions on some unusual local tours or excursions.

RENTING A CAR

Many people prefer to rent a car and explore a new spot at their own pace. It's a chance to spend some quality time with the family or your beloved and absorb the flavor of a port of call. It's a wonderful feeling of independence and relaxation.

Get a map from the rental agency and ask for clear directions to the places you want to visit—and, more important, the way back to the agency. You

144   don't want to spend all your time driving around in
circles!

Some countries may require you to pay a fee, as much
as $25, for a nonresident driver's license (typically valid
for several months). Remember this expense when
deciding whether renting a car is a good way to get
around.

Inspect every inch of your rental car before driving it away. If you see any dents or marks, make
sure they are documented in your contract; otherwise, you will be charged a hefty sum when you
return it.

Check with your credit-card company before you
rent a car—your rental insurance may be covered
by the company, which will save you a lot of money.
Before you drive away, make sure you have the
name and telephone number of the rental agent in
the event you need to call for any reason.

Ask the agent if there are any areas in town that

you should avoid because of construction or crime.

✦

Ask the car-rental agent to point out on the map some residential areas that you can drive through. It's always interesting to check out the neighborhoods in a new port of call and see how people live.

PLAYING IT SAFE WHILE IN PORT

Concerns for safety and security are not limited to the ship. You must always take precautions whenever you step off the ship and into another region of the world. Don't be paranoid, but do be careful and be watchful.

While swimming in the ocean or walking along the beach, wear water socks or other protective footwear. Sea urchins, rock fish, glass, and other "nasties" can be extremely painful—and sometimes deadly—if you accidentally step on them.

✦

When walking around in port, especially in remote and exotic places, try to wash your hands frequently.

146 Drink only bottled water and other beverages, and avoid salads and other fresh vegetables.

In port, be cool—do not make political statements with your clothing. Don't wear T-shirts with religious symbols, flags, and so on.

If you go swimming, snorkeling, or scuba diving, look for posted signs that may caution you about a strong current or undertow. The excursion office onboard the ship can also advise you on safe areas to explore the underwater world.

When scuba diving or snorkeling, never place your hands in a dark hole. An eel may not be too happy having you invade its home!

If you get pricked by a sea urchin, pull the long spikes out of your skin and rub lemon or lime on the area. The acid from these fruits will help dissolve the spikes still embedded in your skin.

If you plan a shore excursion that involves a ride in

a small airplane or helicopter, ask the shore excursion staff about the safety record of the company. It is highly recommended that you book these types of excursions through the cruise line, not on your own.

Never leave valuables like a camera, watch, or Walkman unattended while you are swimming in the ocean. Ask a friend or someone you can trust to watch it for you until you return. If no one's around to assist, seal it in a plastic bag and bury it in the sand under your towel or blanket.

Crowded marketplaces are a haven for pickpockets and thieves. Secure your purse, wallet, and jewelry.

Prepare the payment for your taxi driver while the cabby is driving; don't fumble with a bulging wallet while he looks on.

When visiting areas where animals such as monkeys, birds, snakes, wild pigs, or kangaroos are not

148 in cages, be cautious when petting or feeding them. Even if they appear to be cute and harmless, their bite or scratch could be dangerous.

The ship may be docked overnight in a port. Do not walk around by yourself at night if there are not a lot of people around. Women and seniors especially should avoid walking about in the evening.

When venturing off the ship, attach an identification bracelet on your children with their name, blood type, any chronic illness, medications, allergies, mother's or father's name, telephone number at home, and the telephone number of the ship and the cruise line.

Never carry a wallet in your rear trouser pocket. It is too easy for pickpockets to steal. Keep it in a front pocket of your pants or in an interior pocket of your jacket. A money belt is recommended.

Carry your identification card from the ship.

Instruct your children to contact a clerk in a shop or a police officer if they get lost in port.

Always lock your doors and close your windows when driving around in the ports of call—including in taxis.

HERE'S TO YOUR HEALTH AND WELL-BEING

C RUISE LINES TAKE THE SAFETY and security of their passengers and crew very seriously. Follow the specific guidelines provided to you onboard, and read these tips carefully. They literally can save a life—yours.

SAFETY & SECURITY

They say that rules are meant to be broken, but this is one adage that definitely does not apply at sea. The safety of all people onboard a ship is paramount, and passengers are expected to abide by the rules and regulations established by the particular cruise line as well as by maritime law. I cannot stress it enough: Safety first.

Security is of the utmost importance on cruise ships, especially since the September 11th tragedy. Be patient if you have to go through the same rigorous screening at the pier that you might have experienced at the airport just an hour or two before. Everyone agrees, better to be safe.

152 Let me make one thing perfectly clear: You do not have to worry about the ship capsizing in a storm! They may be tossed around a bit, but cruise ships are built to survive the most severe weather.

The captain will not risk the lives of any passengers or crew members. Should threatening weather or political conditions crop up in a particular port or region, the itinerary of the cruise may be changed. If this happens, go with the flow. Don't grumble—such shifts in plans are made for your safety.

Look around the cabin for any objects that might pose a danger to your little tykes, such as electrical outlets, sharp furniture edges, or things that can be pulled down and hit them on the head. This is usually not a problem on newer ships, but if any hazards are found, contact the cabin steward.

Check the life jackets in your cabin. Are they properly maintained, with a whistle, proper ties, and a light (when the jacket hits salt water, the emergency light attached to the jacket automatically goes on)? Sometimes these items are missing. If this is the case, ask your cabin steward to solve the problem.

Should you detect a fire or smell smoke, don't hesitate—immediately call a crew member or press the nearest fire-alarm switch.

It is unlikely that a person will fall overboard, but if this should happen, throw the nearest life ring into the water and contact a crew member at once.

After participating in the lifeboat drill on the first day of the cruise, look down the hallway near your cabin and locate the closest fire extinguisher and emergency call buttons.

Cabin doors are equipped with special guards or wedges to keep them from swinging open or slamming shut. Use them! You never know when the ship will suddenly list.

154 Never clean your pipe by banging it on the side of the ship. Burning tobacco could blow back onboard and cause a fire. For the same reason, don't throw lit cigarettes or cigars overboard. Put them out in the receptacles provided.

It's best to wear medium-height heels onboard rather than high heels. A sudden movement of the ship could cause you to turn your ankle and become injured.

Use the closets, not the fire sprinklers suspended from the ceiling, to hang your clothing. Garments dangling from the sprinklers could block water from extinguishing a fire in your cabin—obviously, a life-threatening situation for everyone onboard.

Always use the ship's handrails when walking outside on the deck, as a sudden motion of the ship could cause you to lose your balance.

Many doorways and thresholds on the ship have

elevated ledges to cross over. Be extra careful 155 when walking through them.

Make sure that your children know what to do if the emergency signal sounds. The instructions are posted on the back of cabin doors and all around the ship.

In the health club, take special care when using free weights over your head. A sudden movement of the ship could cause you to lose your balance and drop the weights.

Never, *never* make jokes onboard about a bomb scare or a fire. Unfortunately, anyone can be a suspect for terrorism. As in an airport, such "jokes" will be taken seriously, and the crew is likely to hustle you to a security office for questioning. At the very least, this will be unpleasant and embarrassing. You may also be subject to a fine and criminal prosecution. Your children should also understand the serious ramifications of making these kinds of statements.

156 Avoid using the swimming pool if the seas are rough. The force of the waves could push you into the side of the pool and cause a very serious injury. Do not light candles or incense while onboard. This is strictly forbidden by maritime regulations. (If there is candlelight in the dining room, it's never an open flame.)

Should there be an emergency, you will be told where to go. Do not push or shove other passengers, and follow the instructions given by the crew members in charge of the muster station (the place where you gather).

Do not take the elevator during an emergency situation. If for some reason it is hard for you to navigate stairs, contact the information desk and register your name and cabin number on a special emergency-assistance sheet. If something should happen, the crew will come to your cabin and help you to a safe location.

Always use caution when walking on the gangway. Do not feel pressured to walk fast just because other people are waiting behind you. Make sure each step you take is stable, and use the handrails for assistance.

Ask the cabin steward what the wattage is in your cabin or bathroom before plugging in electric razors, toothbrushes, or hair dryers. You don't want to get hurt or cause a fire. If you need a converter, the steward will provide one. Nearly all the newer ships have 110-volt outlets.

It is common for black soot to blow out of the ship's smokestack. Be sure you've checked the deck chairs and lounges before you sit down on them.

Passengers are not allowed to bring visitors onboard. Don't give the security staff on the gangway a hard time when they refuse to let your friends on the ship or check your identification. They are only doing their job, and it's to protect you.

Do not bring illegal drugs onto the ship. If you are

158 caught, you will be released to the local authorities and face criminal charges. Surely experiencing prison life in one of the ports of call is not the sort of sightseeing you have in mind!

In the event that you are harassed by a passenger or crew member, contact the hotel manager and ask for help. Cruise lines will not tolerate such behavior, and the ship's security officers will enforce this policy.

Tell children to contact the nearest crew member should they get lost onboard the ship. An announcement can be made so you can meet them at the information desk.

Lock the door each time you leave your cabin. (If you happen to lock yourself out, the purser's desk will arrange to have someone come by and open the door, or you can ask the nearest cabin steward for a hand.)

Never accept packages from strangers to bring

onto the ship, even if they say that someone 159
onboard is expecting it.

If there is a safe in your cabin, use it to secure your valuables, including your travel documents. If your cabin does not have a safe, ask at the purser's desk to use a safe-deposit box. These boxes are usually available at no extra cost.

MEDICAL CARE

A cruise ship is one place where you don't have to worry about receiving medical attention. Nearly every cruise ship afloat has a full hospital facility, including a pharmacy and X-ray machines, and a professional staff trained to take care of most medical emergencies.

If you expect to need attention from the onboard doctor, be sure you have your medical documents with you. Your cruise agent should also inform the cruise line beforehand that you will be requiring medical assistance while you are onboard.

Tape your name and cabin number on the stems of

160 your eyeglasses and on the inside of their case—thus, in the event you leave them somewhere, lost-and-found will be able to reunite them with you quickly. As an extra precaution, bring a spare pair of glasses or contacts and, if possible, your prescriptions.

People who use oxygen should book direct flights whenever possible, and they should alert the onboard medical personnel as soon as they embark.

If you use the doctor's services or the hospital facility onboard the ship, you will be charged. Your medical insurance should cover this—but be sure to check with your insurance company before leaving on the cruise. Get everything in writing!

Most doctors recommend that pregnant women do not go on a cruise in their third trimester.

Keep your medicine clearly labeled, and bring along copies of your prescriptions.

If you fly through several time zones on your way to joining the ship and you need to take medication at timed intervals, consult your physician or pharmacist to help you plan an easy-to-follow schedule.

Vaccinations may be required if you are traveling to exotic ports of call. Find out from your cruise agent, as you will be required to show proof of your vaccination before embarking.

You can obtain a recent sanitation report of the ship you will be cruising on by contacting the Centers for Disease Control in Washington, D.C., or writing the National Center for Environmental Health, 1015 North American Way, Suite 107, Miami, FL 33132. Inspections are made at least once a year, and for a ship to be in good standing, it must score eighty-six points or higher, out of a possible one hundred.

Being on a cruise ship can motivate you to work out in the health facility, dance the night away in the disco, or participate in an invigorating shore

162 excursion. If you are unaccustomed to regular exercise, take it easy at first!

PREVENTING SEASICKNESS

Seasickness can really place a damper on your cruise. If you think you might be prone to motion sickness, first try a day trip onboard a ship or take a three- or four-day cruise. If you like the idea of a ship but think ocean travel might do you in, opt for a riverboat, steamboat, or barge.

Even old seadogs occasionally get seasick. Be prepared with medicine, and take precautions.

You will help prevent motion sickness if you book a cabin in the center part of the ship—center both horizontally and vertically. (The forward end of the ship, as well as the cabins on the top decks, has more pronounced movement.)

Avoid looking out the window of your cabin or of one of the lounges. The up-and-down motion can make you nauseated.

If you become seasick and your children don't, ask one of the youth counselors onboard to help keep them entertained for the day. They are usually pretty good about that.

Take an antiseasick pill at least two hours before sailing time and throughout the cruise, if needed. If the directions on the medicine say it can cause drowsiness, take half a dose. This will allow you to enjoy the activities and entertainment without being too sleepy.

Most cruise ships are designed with stabilizers, located toward the front of the ship, that extend on both sides just below the waterline. In the event of a storm or rough seas, the stabilizers— as their name implies—help to keep the ship steady.

Some people wear a medicated patch behind their ear to prevent seasickness. Ask your doctor about this option.

Pediatricians should be consulted before the cruise

164   to provide motion-sickness tablets for the kids.

✦

When the seas are rough, don't read a book, write postcards, or do anything else that focuses your attention downward. This may cause you to get seasick.

✦

Old-fashioned cures that sailors have sworn by: If you do begin to feel sick, go outside immediately, take deep breaths, look at the horizon, and stay in the middle section of the ship. Also, eat some dry crackers or bread sticks, and stay away from liquids.

PREVENTING SUNBURN

Too many cruisers have spent their long-awaited vacations lying in bed in helpless torment— burned to a crisp in their zeal to get a tan. Take precautions! There are ways to get a nice glow without doing yourself in.

The sun is very deceiving on a ship. Because the breezes are blowing, keeping you cool, passengers tend to think they are not getting blasted by ultraviolet rays. Always use plenty of sunscreen or sunblock.

In the first couple of days, use a sunblock with a SPF of twenty-five or higher, and do not lie in the sun longer than an hour. You'll get a base of color, but you likely won't be scorched.

Always, always wear a hat!

Passengers have been known to get serious third-degree burns on days when the sky is cloudy. Don't let the overcast sky fool you—wear protection.

Apply sunscreen or sunblock after each dip in the pool or ocean. (Consider getting a spray for quicker application.)

Don't forget to apply sunblock on your lips, ears, and feet!

The beach and poolside are not the only places you

166   have to be concerned about getting a sunburn. Put
on plenty of sunblock when on a shore excursion,
shopping, or strolling onboard.

If you plan to wear strapless or backless evening
wear, apply sunscreen or sunblock during the day
over the appropriate areas so you won't have unat-
tractive tan lines or burns.

When cruising through the Panama Canal or other
regions where the sun's rays are extremely intense,
use an umbrella in addition to sunscreen or sunblock. Temperatures there can reach well over
120° F!

Antarctica cruisers must take special care to protect themselves from ultraviolet rays, as there is
a hole in the ozone layer in that region of the
world.

If you go snorkeling or scuba diving, put extra sunblock on your neck, back, arms, and legs. The sun's
rays can go directly through the water, so wear a T-

shirt to protect your back. Believe me, you'll be grateful you did.

Use aloe vera gel or cream to relieve sunburn pain. Products with aloe vera are also good moisturizers.

CRUISES FOR FAMILIES AND OTHER SPECIAL GROUPS

WHERE CAN WILL AND GRACE, LADIES from the Mother Cabrini Society, specialists in Byzantine archaeology, your globetrotting grandparents from London, and the Osbournes all find the ideal vacation? On a cruise, of course! (Did you really think I'd say something else?) Virtually all kinds of groups can find a cruise that will meet the interests and needs of their members.

Without a doubt, one of the best Web sites I've found is www.cruisegroup.com. Every kind of group is listed under one site. It is certainly my recommendation for information and pricing for anyone or any group looking for people who understand their needs.

FAMILIES

"Family vacation." Sounds like an oxymoron, doesn't it? (Think "honest politician," "military intelligence.") Those who've been there can attest that a holiday with the kids can be more trick than treat.

170   *But families are by far the biggest special-interest group in the cruising industry, and no wonder; it's a wonderful way to travel as a family! Not only is it exciting and exotic, but a cruise can be amazingly inexpensive. Many cruise lines offer family discounts and packages. And the all-inclusive nature of most cruises has a valuable psychological benefit: It relieves that nagging irritation you feel when you are constantly digging into your wallet to pay for a meal—for five.*

Perhaps even more appealing than the financial benefits is that cruising can be so worry-free for parents. There's a lot of space, but the kids can go only the length and breadth of the ship—a secure environment. In addition, many ships offer a cornucopia of facilities and activities that will provide something of interest for everyone. Thus, as the parents sip Campari on their private verandah, serenely watching island peaks go by, their fourteen-year-old is having a blast playing water volleyball, while their ten-year-old goes wild in the video arcade or learns the rudiments of watercoloring.

There are many Web sites specializing in family cruises. The one I found to be the best is www.family

cruisecenter.com, as it offers all kinds of options for 171 those families looking to save money and who still want value.

When you are planning the cruise, include every family member in the discussion. Make a wish list of everyone's choices and communicate the information to your cruise agent.

Family cruises need not be limited to the immediate family, of course. A cruise ship is a great venue for a family reunion. It's also a wonderful way to spend quality time with grandparents, cousins, close family friends, and so on.

Baby-sitting can be arranged at the information desk. Reserve a sitter as soon as you can.

If there are ten or more people traveling from the same city, and you need air transportation to get to the ship, have your cruise agent arrange a group rate with one of the airlines. This could be hundreds of dollars less per person than the cruise line's airfare.

172 If possible, pack each child's belongings in a separate piece of children's luggage.

When packing, remember to bring a favorite stuffed animal, toy, or storybook for each child. This "security blanket" will help the child adjust to the ship.

Put together a "goodie bag" for your children containing projects to occupy them on the plane, while waiting to embark or disembark the ship, and whenever else they may get restless.

Bring along a map of the world. Each night, show your children the places you'll be passing by or visiting the next day. Enrich their understanding of where they're traveling with facts about each place and with historical and cultural information from a travel guidebook.

If your child is not toilet-trained or if you have children under the age of three, they cannot participate in the youth program provided by the cruise line. However, baby-sitting services are available.

Cruise ships are very different from most people's 173 surroundings in normal life. To help your children feel comfortable, walk around the ship with them after unpacking and get familiar with the facilities.

Even eight-year-olds enjoy the thrill of spending recklessly. Give your children some money to blow on their vacation.

Ask one of the kids to be responsible for assembling a family scrapbook of the cruise, with photos, ticket stubs, excursion brochures, and so on.

To lend structure to the cruise, assign each child a chore. An older sibling might baby-sit the twins late at night while the parents boogie in the disco. For their part, the twins can put away all the kids' toys and clothes each evening before bed.

Have some brightly colored T-shirts with the name of the ship or some special symbol (for security reasons, no kids' names, please) made up for each family member. Not only will this serve as a nice

174 memento, but it will help you find each other at a glance, onboard and off.

Most cruise lines that focus on family cruising will have cribs available. If you need one for your baby, ask your cruise agent to request one for you.

If the family is in two or more cabins, buy a pair of walkie-talkies so you can communicate back and forth, both on the ship and in a busy shopping port. It'll be fun for the kids and will help you keep track of everyone.

Most ships offer a parent/child orientation with the youth supervisors on the first day of the cruise. The staff will provide detailed information about the programs and help the kids choose those that are right for them.

Give the children some basic rules of etiquette to follow when they are onboard the ship. (The last thing you want is the management calling to complain about your child's behavior.) Emphasize the importance of the safety instructions.

The drinking age onboard most cruise ships is eighteen, because the ships will be sailing in international waters. Teenagers should know that they will be asked for an ID if they order alcohol.

Keep a note pad in the cabin so everyone can record where they can be found throughout the day.

Some cruise lines let children travel free if they stay in their parents' cabin. This will not be very appealing for some couples (or for their kids, for that matter), but for those who expect to use the cabin as a mere pit stop, it's a great deal!

❀

When the ship is in port, older teenagers who want to venture off by themselves should be given a designated time and place to meet with their parents. All family members should know the name of the ship in case they get lost.

❀

The cruise program for the following day arrives in your cabin the preceding evening. At bedtime, plan the next day's schedule with the children. Find at

176 least one activity that the entire family can participate in together. Also insist that everyone meet for dinner. It may be the only time you'll be all together during the cruise.

❖

If your cabins are next to wild party-givers or particularly loud lovers, you might want to ask the hotel manager if it is possible to be moved. Along the same lines, expect courtesy from the kids—don't let them disturb their neighbors. They shouldn't be allowed to shriek, run in and out slamming doors, jump on the beds, pound on walls, and so on.

❖

Hand-draw a simple map of the ship for younger children so it is easier for them to find their cabin. Also, let them tape a little drawing to the outside of their cabin door so they can see their cabin from way down the hall.

SINGLES

In recent years, cruise lines have put together many packages meant to appeal particularly to single people. Singles are a unique breed of cruisers. They are often exceptionally adventur-

ous, joining in many activities with zeal and good 177
humor. Sometimes people without partners opt
for a cruise geared toward singles because they
often feel excluded in our couples-oriented soci-
ety; on the cruise—or at least in various programs
and activities—they can be among the majority for
a change. And, not surprisingly, given the inher-
ently sensual nature of cruising, many singles are
looking for a little romance on the Love Boat. Or,
even better, some "motion on the ocean." Olé!

Sometimes single passengers can cruise at a
lower rate during the off seasons. Ask your cruise
agent to look into these fares.

Beware of ship's officers who make marriage pro-
posals or make you feel like you are the love of
their life. Chances are they used the same line on
another passenger on the cruise before—if not the
night before! Enjoy their attentions by all means,
but be realistic.

If you are accustomed to a queen- or king-size bed
at home, ask the cabin steward to push the twin

178 beds together. You'll be more comfortable, and who knows, you just may need the extra room for a romantic occasion later in the cruise.

If you are an older single man, you might qualify to cruise for free or at a considerable discount as a gentleman host. You can find out more about this program by calling the cruise lines directly.

If you don't want to be bothered by other passengers looking for a date, wear a wedding ring. This should keep most (but probably not all!) potential love interests away.

Opt for elegance rather than exhibitionism in your clothing. Extremely provocative swimwear and evening wear will likely attract more pests than princes.

If you are interested in meeting other single passengers, ask the maitre d' to seat you at a dining table with single guests.

GAYS AND LESBIANS

The gay and lesbian cruise travel market has tripled in the past decade. Many cruise lines make a special effort to design packages that will appeal to people with nontraditional life-styles.

There are many companies that offer gay and lesbian cruises, like Olivia Cruises and RSVP. Before you book your cruise directly with them, you may want to check out www.fairyboat.com. This company will not only discount your trip, regardless of whether it's on a gay or lesbian cruise or with a major cruise line, but they will also donate 10 percent of their commission to any AIDS organization of your choice.

Buy a gay/lesbian guidebook, like *Spartacus International Gay Guide* or a Bob Damron guidebook, before leaving on your cruise. The information in these books will provide a list of gay restaurants and other facilities in the ports of call you'll be visiting.

180 Ask the shore excursion staff if they can recommend different places in port that you can explore. Many times they will know of gay establishments.

Be patient, not angry or rude, to passengers who frown upon your homosexuality or bother you in any way.

When you arrive onboard the ship, ask the cruise director to help you set up a gathering. Ask her to print in the daily program: "Friends of Dorothy's get-together" or "pink-triangle party." Most homosexuals will understand this code and come to the festivities to meet other gay people early in the cruise.

SENIORS

Many older people today have not only the time but also the financial resources to cruise the world in style—and many are doing so. Two-week, two-month, even six-month cruises to exotic ports of call around the world beckon to these discerning travelers.

Generally speaking, the longer the cruise, the older the passengers onboard the ship.

Some cruise lines sail more seniors than others.

If you are looking for a relaxing cruise with no children running around the ship, ask your cruise agent to suggest a couple of options.

When cruising during a holiday, you can expect several hundred children (or more!) to be onboard many of the larger cruise ships.

If you are used to going to bed or eating dinner early, start adjusting your clock to the ship's schedule a month before you go on your cruise.

Don't be afraid to talk to passengers of all ages. One of the advantages of a cruise is the opportunity to meet all sorts of people, of all ages—and for them to have the pleasure of getting to know you.

If you are dancing with one of the gentleman hosts

182 or cruise staff, remember that they are onboard the ship for your dancing pleasure only!

Beware of pushy taxi drivers in some ports of call. They may promise a certain fare and then try to take advantage of you because you're a senior citizen. Try to establish a fare in advance (in some countries, the government sets the rates). If the cabby goes over that fare, get one of the port agents to sort out the conflict.

HONEYMOONERS & ROMANTICS

A kiss on the cheek while strolling on the deck and an intense gaze across the dining-room table are just a couple of the subtle ways honeymooners and romantics express their affection when sailing onboard a love boat. Cruising is the ideal vacation for those who want to enhance or rekindle their relationships.

There are three terrific Internet sites that offer honeymoon cruises at a discount: www.honeymoonsrus. com, www.davidsbridalhoneymoon.com, and www. romanticsea.com. All these companies are bonded

and accredited, and they provide professional staff 183
who take time to work within your budget and special needs.

A great way to begin your cruise, and a nice way to say "I love you" to the person you will be cruising with, is to order a bon voyage gift and have it waiting in the cabin when you arrive on the ship. Ask your cruise agent to arrange the gift.

Everyone loves a lover—within reason. Spare your fellow passengers the details of your sex life. They really are not interested in watching you make out in the pool or writhe against each other on the dance floor.

If you want to impress your special someone, ask your cruise agent or the shore excursion staff to inquire about limousine service in one of the ports of call. It's a great feeling to walk down a gangway in a glamorous island port and know that the shiny limousine is all yours, waiting to escort you and your loved one around the island in utter comfort. Go all the way—arrange to have strawberries and champagne waiting inside!

184 If you are fairly recently married or have different last names, bring along a copy of your marriage certificate for immigration. You may need it as a form of identification.

Where better to get married than on a glorious cruise ship? Ask your cruise agent to inquire with the cruise line about this option for tying the knot.

Sometimes you can get married on land and have the reception onboard while the ship is docked in port. Your guests will be thrilled, and once they leave, you and your sweetheart can begin your honeymoon. Your cruise agent can help with the arrangements.

If you wear your wedding dress to the ship, ask the cruise director if it can be stored in one of the costume areas. Usually there is room, and it can hang there, protected and secure, until you disembark.

Your cruise agent can help you arrange to renew your wedding vows onboard the ship. (If you feel impassioned once onboard, the cruise director may also be able to assist you!) Many cruise ships now have an onboard wedding chapel. If you would like to get married onboard a ship, your cruise agent can arrange the ceremony through the cruise line's special wedding department. There is usually a $1,000 price tag for a basic wedding onboard the ship.

Ask your cabin steward to place a red rose on your partner's pillow when preparing your cabin for the evening. Include a note written by you suggesting a bit of fun and frolic. (Don't forget to give your cabin steward a couple of dollars for helping out.)

Sit in the Jacuzzi late at night with a bottle of champagne, a bowl of strawberries, and some soft music. Ask your cabin steward to help arrange the setup. (A nice tip would be appropriate here).

If you know your loved one's favorite song, talk to the musicians beforehand and have them play the song while you enjoy a cocktail or dance in one of the lounges. The cruise director can also arrange this.

186 Take a walk outside late at night and steal a kiss in the moonlight. If the fireworks start exploding, go to your cabin—do not attempt to climb into one of the lifeboats!

If your cabin has a verandah or balcony, request dinner to be brought to your stateroom, and dine outside with your special someone. It is very romantic!

Buy each other something special in the onboard gift or jewelry shop to remember the wonderful time together.

PEOPLE WITH SPECIAL NEEDS

Most cruise ships are wheelchair-friendly, and so are the crew and staff who work on them. Don't hesitate for one minute if you are physically or otherwise challenged and worried about whether you will be all right on a cruise. Go for it, and have the time of your life!

Not all cruise ships are built to accommodate physically challenged passengers. The newer vessels,

though, have terrific cabins, and it is easy to access
all areas of the ship. Make sure your cruise agent
has specifically asked the cruise line about this,
and get confirmation in writing.

Most cruise lines require physically challenged
passengers to sail with an able-bodied companion.
Be sure that the person you are traveling with under-
stands the responsibilities before getting onboard
the ship.

If you don't have a traveling companion, call your
local hospital and ask if there are any retired
nurses or aides who might be interested in going
with you. You will have no problem finding one—
especially, of course, if you are paying for the
cruise.

Some cruise lines allow seeing-eye dogs onboard
their ships, but you must get written permission in
advance. Your cruise agent can arrange this.

A limited number of wheelchair-accessible cabins
are available on cruise ships. Try to make your cruise

188 travel arrangements at least a year in advance.

If you are hearing-impaired, make sure your cruise companion lets you know about any important onboard announcements.

The Society for the Advancement of Travel for the Handicapped (SATH) offers advice to people with handicaps who wish to travel. Call (212) 447–7284 for a free copy of SATH's newsletter.

Inform the hotel staff of your disability. In the event of an emergency, a special rescue party will go to your cabin and assist in taking you to your emergency boat station.

If you are physically challenged, contact the cruise director. The cruise staff will then be informed, and you can feel more comfortable about participating in entertainment and activities.

It is very difficult for passengers in wheelchairs to

go ashore when the ship is tendering. The staff at 189
the information desk can help arrange preboarding
for you or set up a better time for you to use the
tender boats.

On bus tours in ports of call, often a tour guide
explains the sights over a microphone system.
Remember this when booking excursions if you are
hearing-impaired.

BUSINESS MEETINGS, CLUBS, AND LARGER GROUPS

*I can't think of a better place to hold a business
meeting than in a conference room onboard a
cruise ship. Where else can you watch the head
speaker stand at a podium and sway from side to
side? Cruise ships are equipped with the latest
technologies that allow nearly any kind of group,
business committee, or club to gather together
and conduct business. Next time your organization wants to hold a big meeting, suggest a cruise
ship!*

Large groups can receive a substantial discount on

190 a cruise. Have your cruise agent contact the group department at the cruise line you wish to sail with. Have your cruise agent arrange with the cruise line to set up a desk in the lobby area on the ship. This will give everyone traveling in your group a focal point and central area in which to meet.

Ask your cruise agent to book a section of cabins in the same general area of the ship. This will give you an opportunity to keep some cabin doors open and visit from cabin to cabin. (Remember to respect the privacy and quiet times of those not involved in your party.)

Your cruise agent and the group department of the cruise line will be able to advise you on specific arrangements for conferences, seminars, dinners, and so on. It is no more complicated than arranging a group meeting or conference on land—but it is so much more memorable and satisfying an event!

Family reunions, corporate business meetings, high school reunions, and all kinds of large groups are choosing a cruise as their venue for meeting. For 191 information on how you can design a cruise that best suits the needs of your large group, contact www.cruisedesigners.com. They have a wonderful staff who works with you personally to see that every detail is covered.

Fund-raising is important to many nonprofit organizations, churches, schools, and families in a financial crisis. If your organization is interested in a cruise fund-raiser, contact www.cruiseaid.com. They'll arrange the details and show you how you can make thousands of dollars to help you with your "crusade."

Have identifying tags, T-shirts, or other mementos made in advance and pass them out to the group members as they arrive onboard.

Contact the ship's photographer to organize a group photograph.

WHEN THE PARTY'S OVER

YOU'VE EATEN YOUR LAST SUPPER, sat on your suitcase to get it shut, and hidden your new diamond necklace in the dirty laundry to try to beat the customs man. Ready or not, it's time to go home.

Don't be too sad—as my grandma used to say, "If you don't leave, how can you come back again?" That said, it is true that you will probably feel a little blue. But you'll have happier memories of the cruise as a whole if you take a few simple steps to make the transfer home more relaxed and your readjustment to real life less jarring.

PACKING UP

It will be a lot easier to pack up at the end of the cruise than it was to pack for the cruise. Since you will probably be cleaning all your clothes when you get home, wrinkling and organization won't be such an issue. Go ahead—throw everything in pronto so that you can enjoy every last minute of your adventure!

194 Don't forget to gather all your personal items from your cabin safe or from the safe-deposit box at the purser's desk. If you forget something on the ship, contact the cruise line's corporate office. (Unfortunately, not all items are turned into the lost-and-found, so remember to check everywhere before you leave.)

You will be asked to place your luggage outside your cabin door the night before disembarkation; the ship's staff will take it to a central area for distribution. Make sure you have kept a change of clothing for the following day—you don't want to walk down the gangway wrapped in a shower curtain!

Roll up each piece of dirty laundry as tightly as possible and place it around any breakable items (some of these items you might prefer to carry with you).

Pack all valuables in your carry-on bags.

DISEMBARKATION

Getting the passengers and luggage off the ship is typically a long and tiring process because the ship has to get clearance from the port authorities and you may have to go through immigration and customs. Instead of getting frustrated, use the time to take a last stroll around the ship, enjoy a good-bye conversation with your new friends, and admire the views of the port where the ship has docked.

A day or so before you leave the ship, the cruise director will hold a briefing, explaining all the procedures to follow regarding disembarkation. At least one person from each family should attend this talk, as the information will provide a smooth transition for you to leave the ship. This briefing will also give you an opportunity to ask questions. Bring a paper and pen and note the most important points.

❁

You can realistically count on two to three hours of waiting around before the actual disembarkation from the ship begins. Keep a crossword puzzle,

196 cards, or a book handy to amuse yourself during
this time.

Physically challenged passengers and any other
guests needing assistance are given priority disembarkation privileges. Please don't abuse this
privilege if you don't really qualify for it.

If you are on the air-sea package, you will be
transferred to the airport by the cruise-line repre-
sentatives. The earlier your flight, the sooner you
will disembark from the ship and be transferred.

On the morning of disembarkation, breakfast hours
will be moved back one hour. This will be your last
opportunity to eat before leaving the ship, so if you
want breakfast, plan on getting up early.

Passengers are not allowed to disembark from the
ship until all the luggage has been taken off the
vessel and arranged in the terminal building, usually according to a number or colored tag that you
placed on your bags the night before. This proce-

dure can take a good couple of hours. Be patient! 197
Getting irritated won't speed it along.

✲

Porters will be available in the luggage terminal to help you transfer your bags. It is customary to tip these gentlemen $1.00 per bag.

✲

Sometimes passengers leave a ship and their cruise with a bad impression because the disembarkation process was too long or poorly organized. You can help the cruise line and yourself if you eat a leisurely breakfast, relax in your cabin or one of the public lounges, and plan an activity to amuse yourself until it is time to leave.

✲

Don't gather around the gangway area and talk to the staff in charge of helping with disembarkation. Letting them get their job done will speed the process for everyone. You'll have plenty of other opportunities to say good-bye.

✲

Room service and bar service are discontinued on the morning of disembarkation.

198 When the captain receives clearance from the port authorities, disembarkation can begin. In some cases, not only will you have to wait for this clearance, but you will also have to pass through customs.

If there is a "lucky comment-card drawing" at the end of your cruise, make sure you enter. Sometimes cruise lines give away a discount on a future cruise. Also, be as honest as you can with your comments—the cruise lines will appreciate any advice you can give to better their product.

AFTER YOUR CRUISE

When your cruise is finished, you arrive home and begin your re-entry into real life. Slowly, you will begin to get into your daily routine again—whether you want to or not. But something will feel different. You'll find that you are craving something unlike anything you've ever hungered for before. It isn't a sick feeling, but an overpowering sense of want, desire, and obsession. It is a condition called cruise-itis. (The technical name is "frequent floaters disease.") The symptoms?

You can't stop talking about your cruise. You thrive on other people's cruise stories, and you even look for ways to top them. You go to your cruise agent, start looking at cruise brochures again, and begin planning your next cruise.

This phase is very common, and the symptoms last only a couple of weeks. Many people go through it, so don't panic. Eventually you will get back to normal and will even enjoy your "real" life again. You'll gradually become your old self—that is, until the next cruise.

If you are on a post-land package, you may begin your tour immediately after you disembark from the ship. This means you may not see your hotel until that evening. Make sure you have had a good breakfast, are wearing comfortable clothing and shoes, and have had a stop at the rest room before the tour.

Some cruise agents do a tremendous amount of work to see that you have the best cruise possible. If you thoroughly enjoyed your cruise, why not send a thank-you note or perhaps give your agent

200 a souvenir from one of the ports of call? These gestures are really appreciated.

❄

Call the cruise agency or e-mail them with feedback about your cruise, good and bad. This helps them to know whether or not to recommend that cruise ship or cruise line again.

❄

Join the cruise line's repeat-passenger club. On your next cruise with that cruise line, you'll receive some nice gifts, an invitation to a special cocktail party, and early check-in at the pier.

❄

If you were happy with the service you received from one particular staff member, write a letter to the cruise-line corporate office and commend the cruise line for hiring such a professional person. These letters carry a tremendous amount of weight, especially when there is a possibility of promotion of a crew member.

❄

If your cruise was a complete disaster, explain the details to your cruise agent. She will contact the cruise line and attempt to get some kind of discount or refund, if the situation merits. If you feel your cruise agent was the reason for the disaster, use the tips in the section on planning your cruise to find a different cruise agent for next time.

Ask your cruise agent to let you know about discounts on future cruises.

Share your good fortune. An organization called A New Voyage gives children who have successfully completed treatments for a serious illness the chance to experience a complimentary cruise. If you would like to donate to this worthwhile, non-profit organization in order to help fund the airline flights, port charges, taxes, transfers, and other cruise-related expenses, write to A New Voyage, 117 West Saint Paul Street, Spring Valley, IL 61362-0147.

If you are interested in becoming a cruise agent yourself and would like to take a cruise course on-line, go to www.cruisecourse.com. It is a wonderful way to supplement your income and also receive substantial discounts on future cruises.

202 FINDING EMPLOYMENT ON CRUISE SHIPS

On every cruise, at least fifty people ask me about employment opportunities onboard a ship. While it is wonderful to work on a cruise ship, it is not suited for everyone. Cruise lines hire professionals, not individuals that want to get away from their boring job at home and work for a couple of weeks or months. Working onboard a ship is completely different from vacationing on one. It takes high energy, strong commitment, and long hours.

Some cruise lines receive 200 to 300 photos and résumés each month from people seeking employment. Because the demand is so great, the employees who work on cruise ships must be extremely service-oriented and have brilliant customer-service skills. They must also have some kind of training or experience in the department in which they hope to work.

If you are seriously interested in working onboard a cruise ship, contact the Cruise Staff Training Institute. You can e-mail them at cruising@ivnet.com for information.

Working on a cruise ship is not as glamorous as you might think. But if you like people, are willing to work long hours, and love the sea, then working on a ship may be the perfect career.

✦

Beware of scam operators promising jobs on cruise ships. No one can promise you a job except the cruise line itself. Before you order any type of book regarding employment opportunities on cruise ships, ask for the copyright date, the name and reputation of the author, and detailed information about its contents. Sometimes, even if the book has 300 pages, only 20 of those pages are related to cruise ships, and even those pages could be outdated or irrelevant.

✦

To begin a career on a cruise ship, it is imperative that you learn the basics. Order *The Complete Cruise Ship Employment Package* for $49.05 plus $5.00 shipping. Fax orders to Cruise Concepts Inc. at (815) 663-3131.

About the Author

Jim West is one of the most sought-after and foremost authorities on cruise travel today. He has sailed on over 850 cruises, explored all seven continents (yes, even Antarctica), and has traveled to sixty-four countries around the world. As a cruise director he has given advice to over one million people. He has worked onboard the ships of Celebrity Cruises, Princess Cruises, Orient Lines, and Fantasy Cruises for a combined total of ten years.

Jim is a contributing author of the newly released *Chicken Soup for the Traveler's Soul,* as well as author of three other best-selling cruise travel books. He has been recommended by and featured on radio programs and television shows and in many major newspapers and magazines, including the *Los Angeles Times, Cruise Travel Magazine,* the *Chicago Tribune,* and *Honeymoon Magazine,* just to name a few.

One only needs to go on-line to Google and type in "cruise expert Jim West" to discover that he is known far and wide for his cruise expertise. He has received notes of thanks from movie stars, sports celebrities, and even the former King and Queen of Greece, who praised his ability as a cruise director. Jim is happy to speak with anyone regarding cruises they might be interested in planning. Phone toll-free (888) 867–8600 or e-mail him at travel@travelwest.com.